IRON MAIDEN
A MATTER OF LIFE AND DEATH

GUITAR TAB EDITION

DIFFERENT WORLD 2
THESE COLOURS DON'T RUN 12
BRIGHTER THAN A THOUSAND SUNS 22
THE PILGRIM 33
THE LONGEST DAY 41
OUT OF THE SHADOWS 51
THE REINCARNATION OF BENJAMIN BREEG 58
FOR THE GREATER GOOD OF GOD 70
LORD OF LIGHT 85
THE LEGACY 98

Published by
Wise Publications
14-15 Berners Street, London, W1T 3LJ, UK.

Exclusive distributors:
Music Sales Limited
Distribution Centre, Newmarket Road,
Bury St Edmunds, Suffolk, IP33 3YB, UK.

Music Sales Pty Limited
120 Rothschild Avenue, Rosebery,
NSW 2018, Australia.

Order No. AM988086
ISBN 1-84609-810-6
This book © Copyright 2006 Wise Publications,
a division of Music Sales Limited.

Unauthorised reproduction of any part of
this publication by any means including photocopying
is an infringement of copyright.

Edited by Tom Farncombe.
Music arranged by Martin Shellard.
Music processed by Paul Ewers Music Design.

www.musicsales.com

Your Guarantee of Quality:
As publishers, we strive to produce every book
to the highest commercial standards.

The music has been freshly engraved and
the book has been carefully designed to minimise
awkward page turns and to make playing from it a real
pleasure. Particular care has been given to specifying
acid-free, neutral-sized paper made from pulps which
have not been elemental chlorine bleached.

This pulp is from farmed sustainable forests
and was produced with special regard for
the environment.

Throughout, the printing and binding have
been planned to ensure a sturdy, attractive
publication which should give years of enjoyment.

If your copy fails to meet our high standards,
please inform us and we will gladly replace it.

This publication is not authorised for sale in
the United States of America and/or Canada

WISE PUBLICATIONS
part of The Music Sales Group
London / New York / Paris / Sydney / Copenhagen / Berlin / Madrid / Tokyo

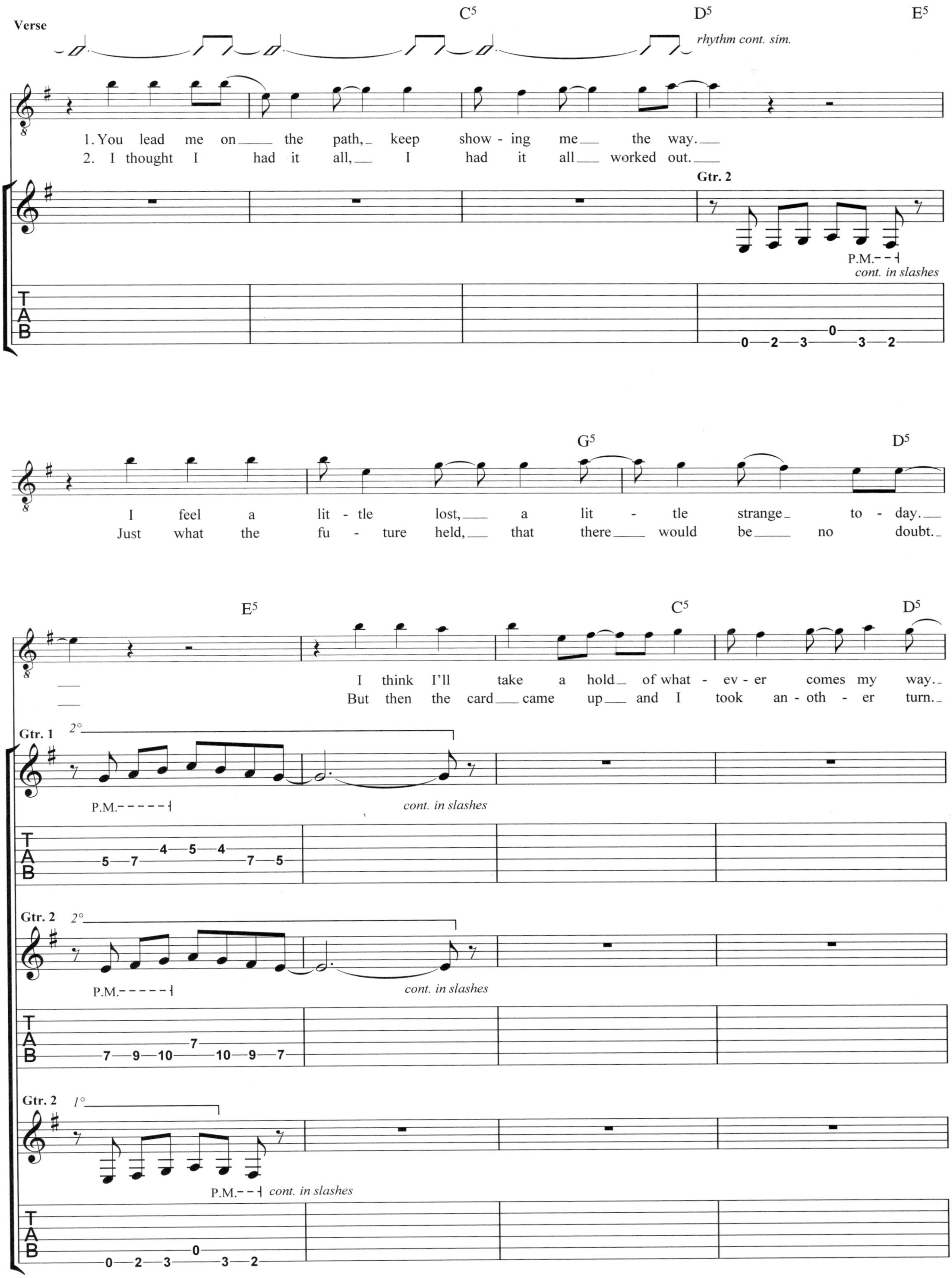
Verse
C5
D5
E5
rhythm cont. sim.
1. You lead me on the path, keep show - ing me the way.
2. I thought I had it all, I had it all worked out.
Gtr. 2
P.M.
cont. in slashes
T
A
B
G5
D5
I feel a lit - tle lost, a lit - tle strange to - day.
Just what the fu - ture held, that there would be no doubt.
E5
C5
D5
I think I'll take a hold of what - ev - er comes my way.
But then the card came up and I took an - oth - er turn.
Gtr. 1
2°
P.M.
cont. in slashes
Gtr. 2
2°
P.M.
cont. in slashes
Gtr. 2
1°
P.M.
cont. in slashes

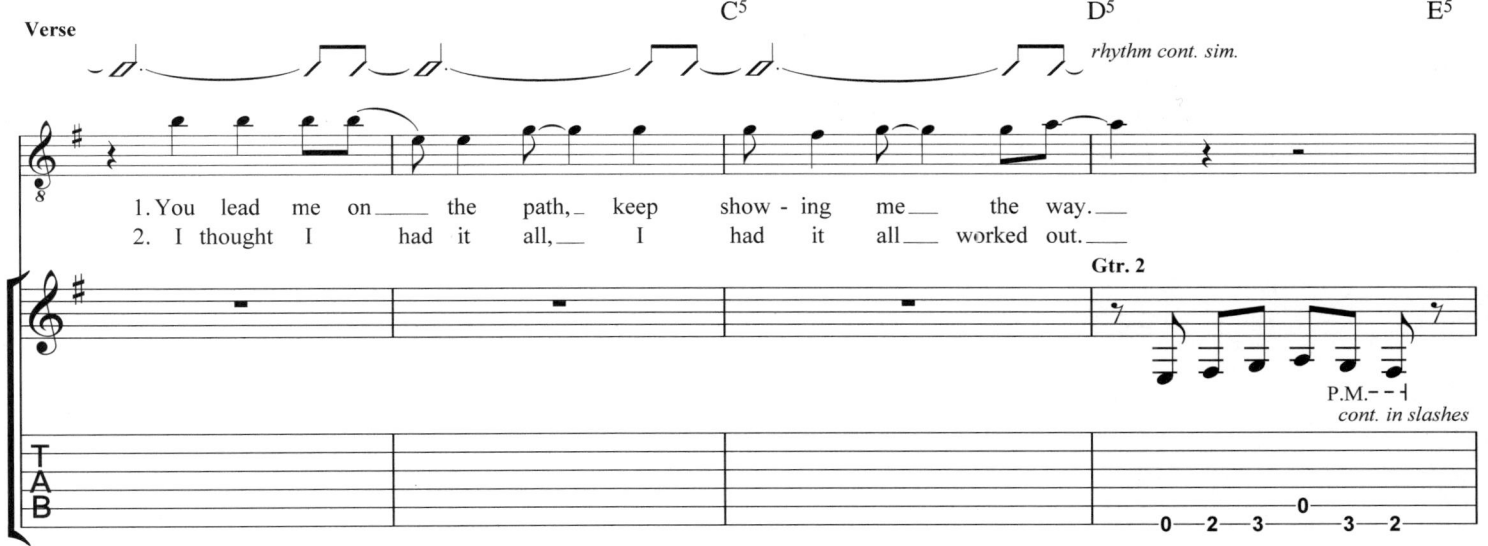

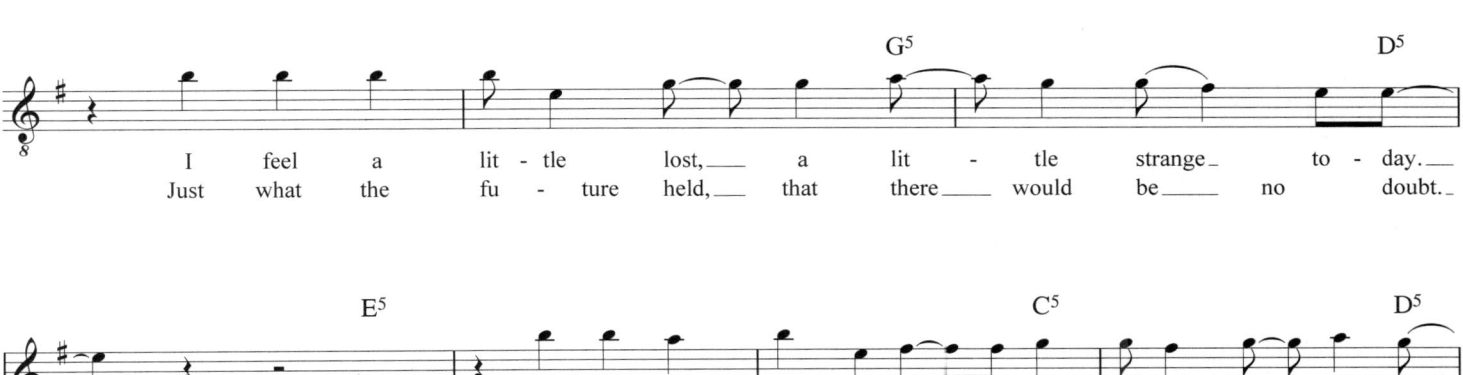

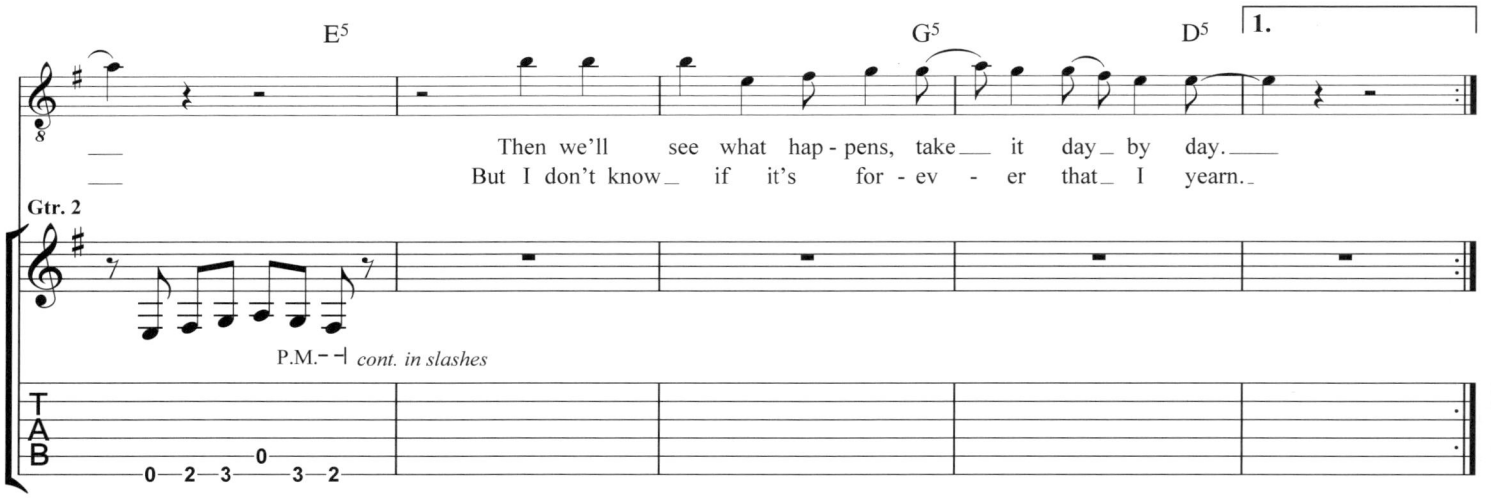
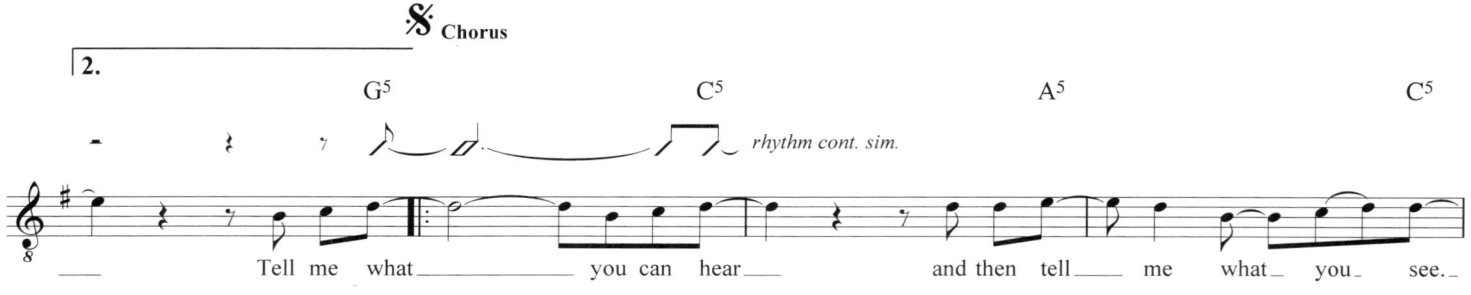

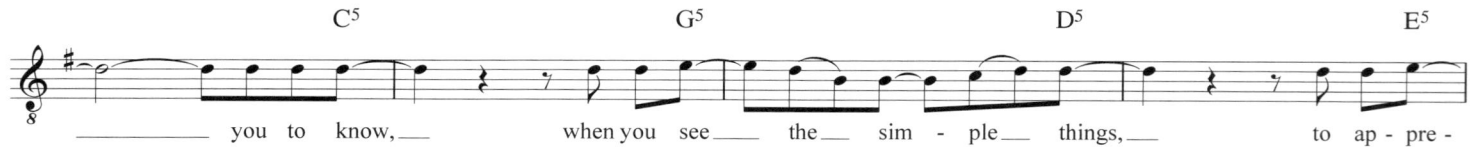

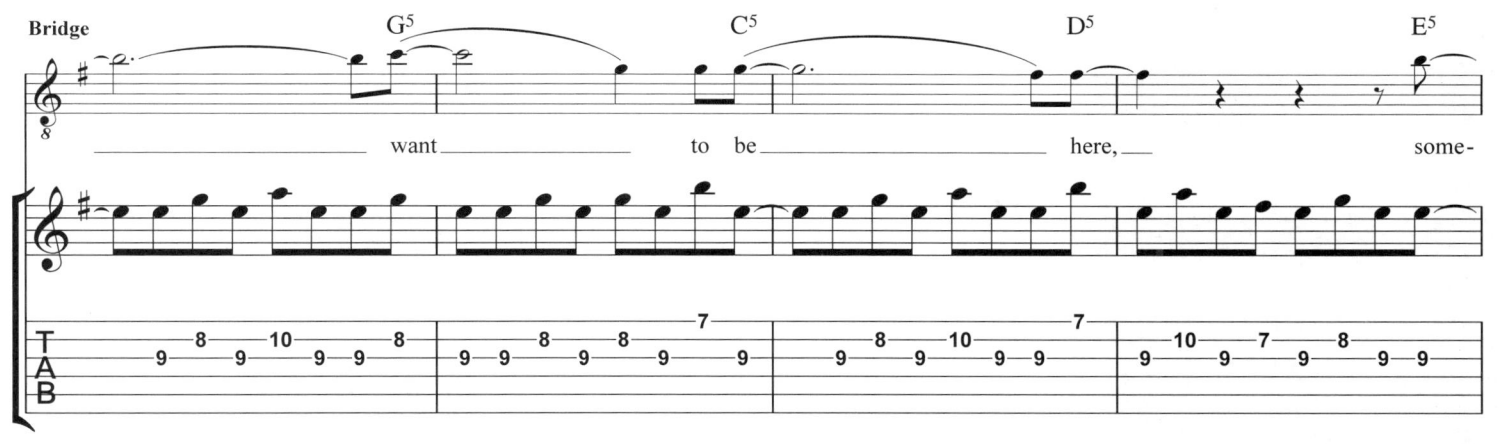
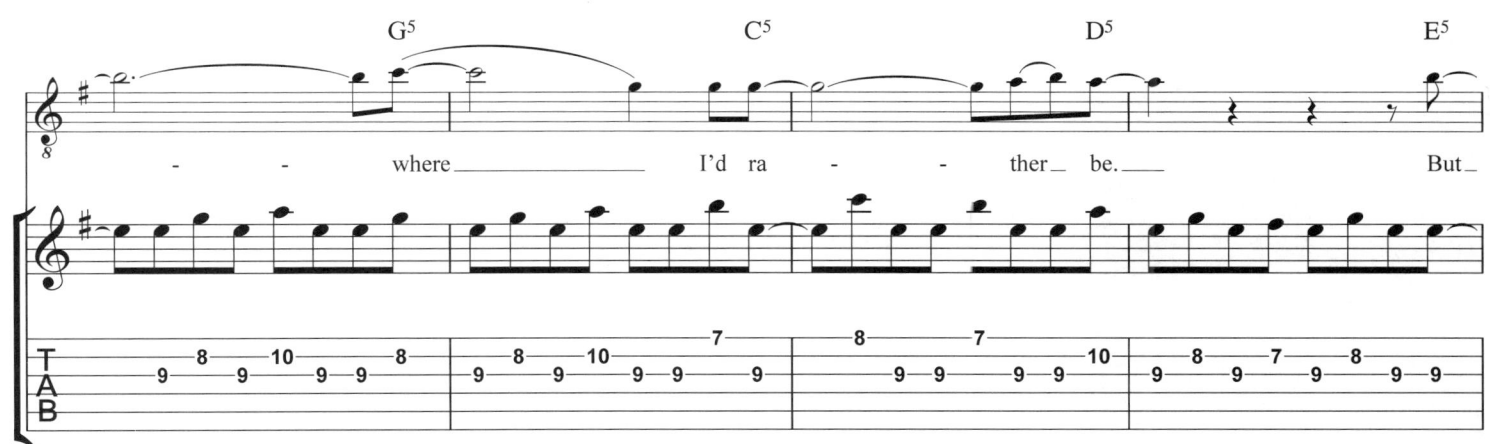
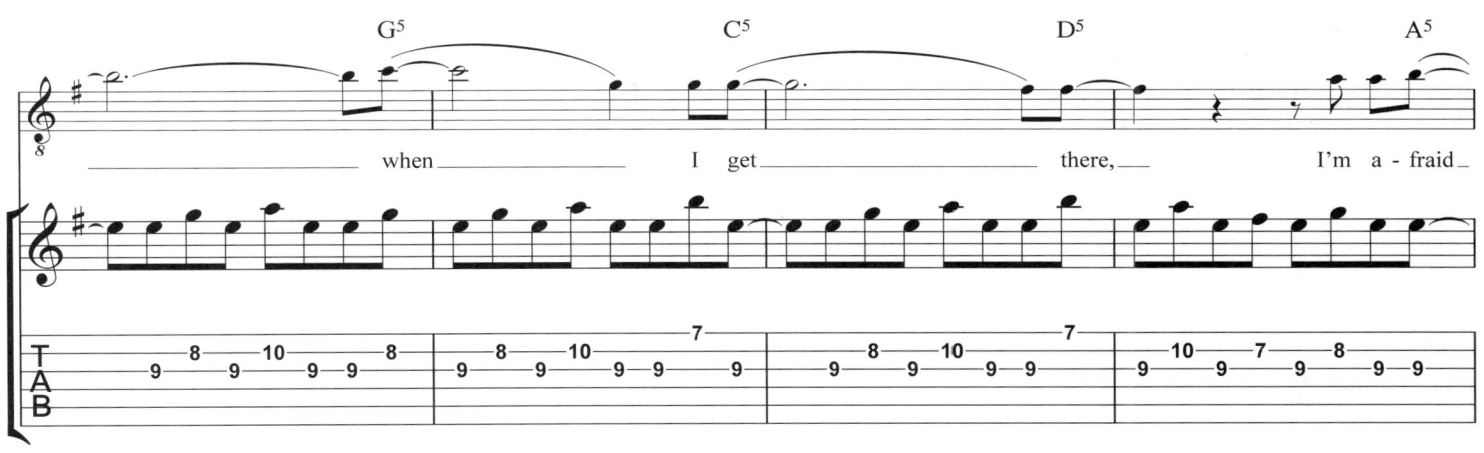
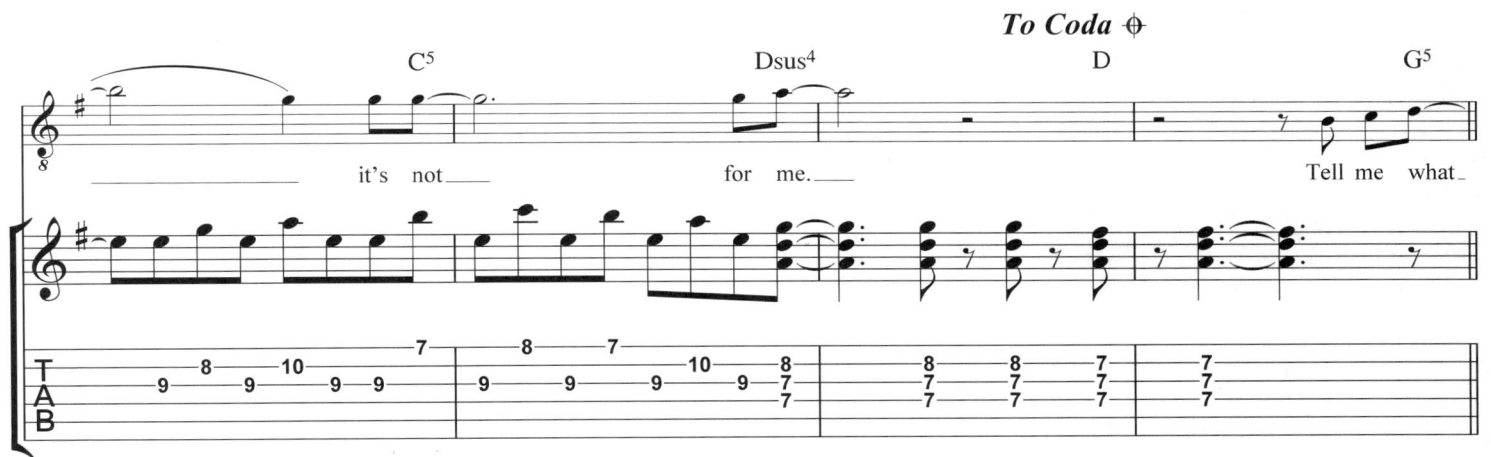

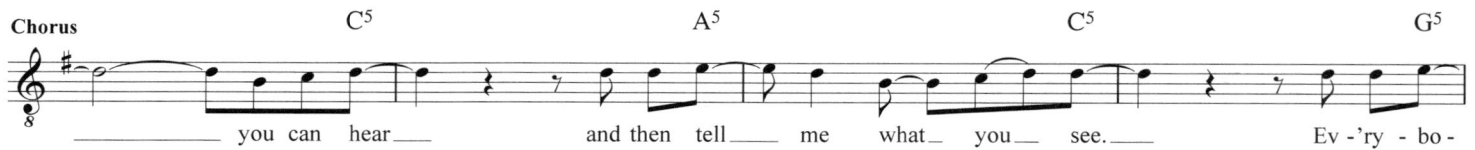
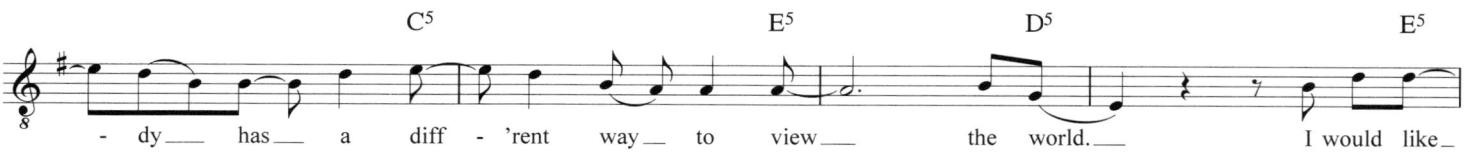
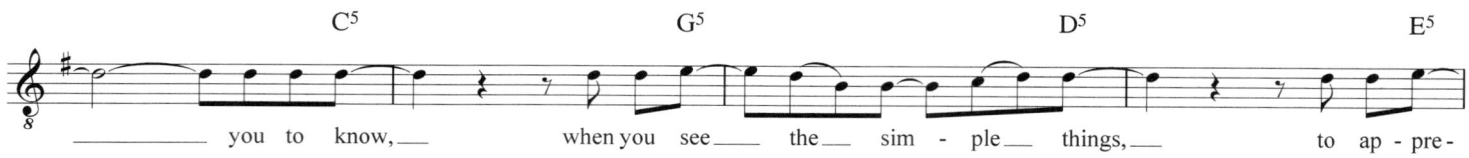

E5
C5
G5
D5
E5
C5
G5
D5
Gtr. 4
f w/dist.

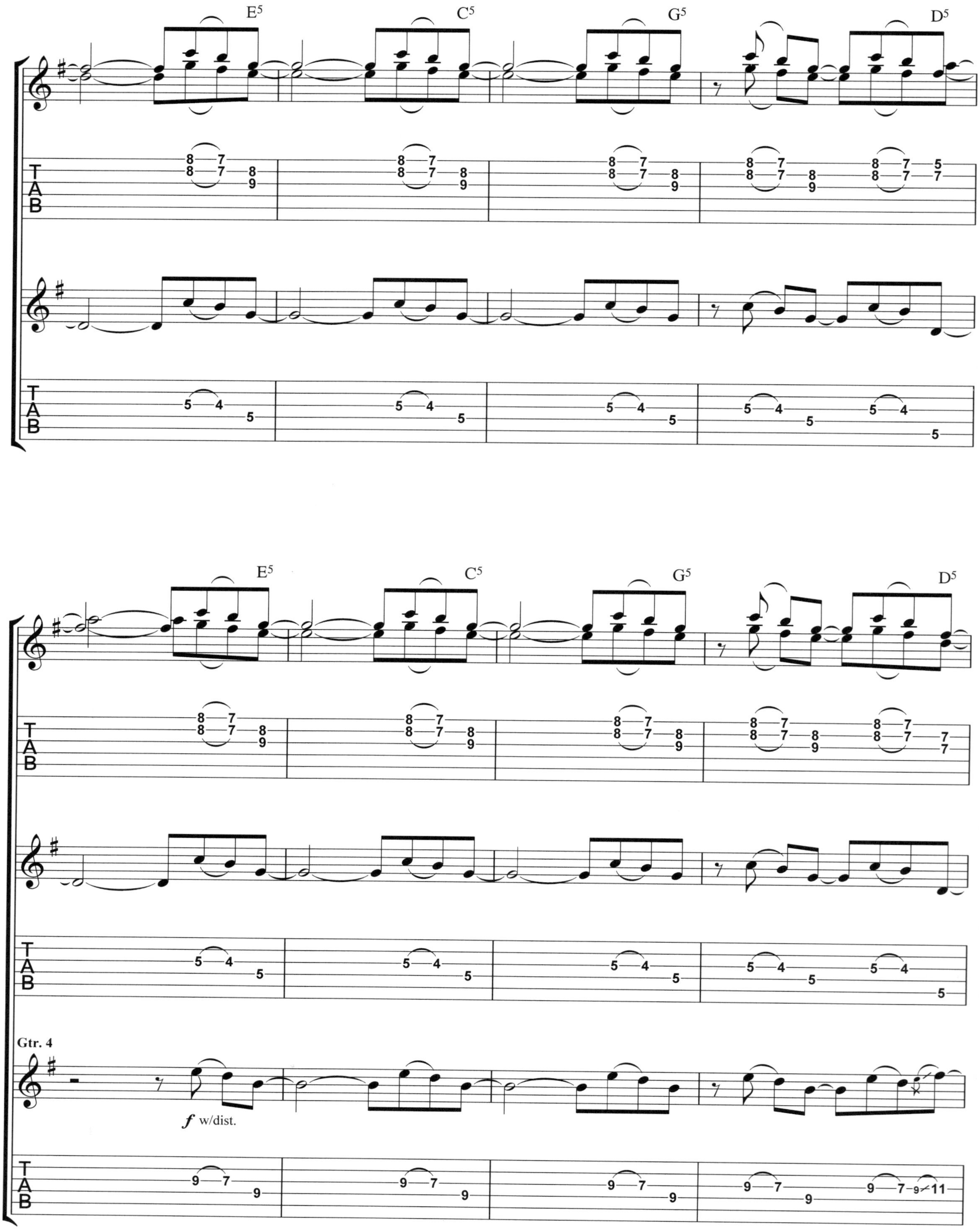

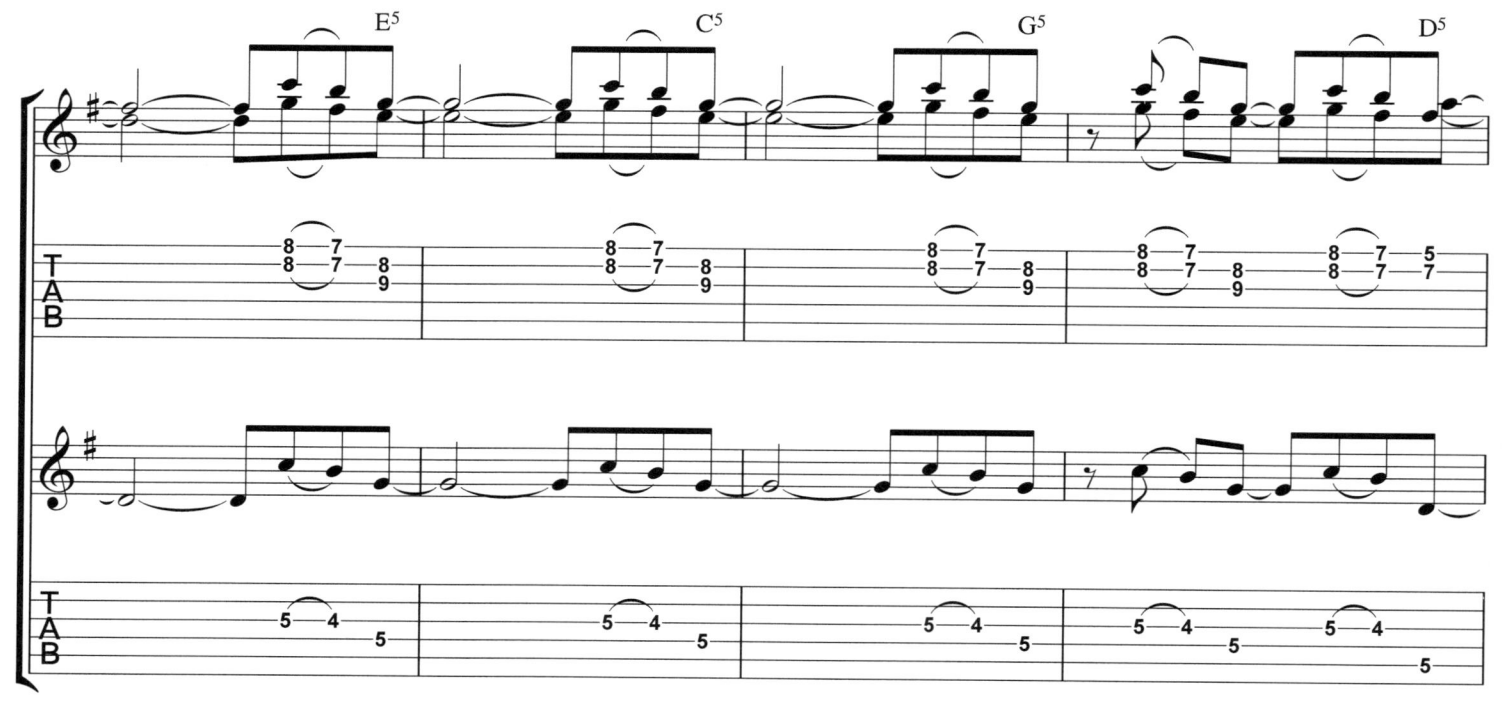

E5
Gtrs. 1+2
A5
C5
D5
Gtr. 5
cont. in slashes
f w/dist.
1/2
Gtr. solo
C5
G5
D5
E5
rhythm cont. sim.
Gtrs. 3+4 tacet
full
C5
G5
D5
E5

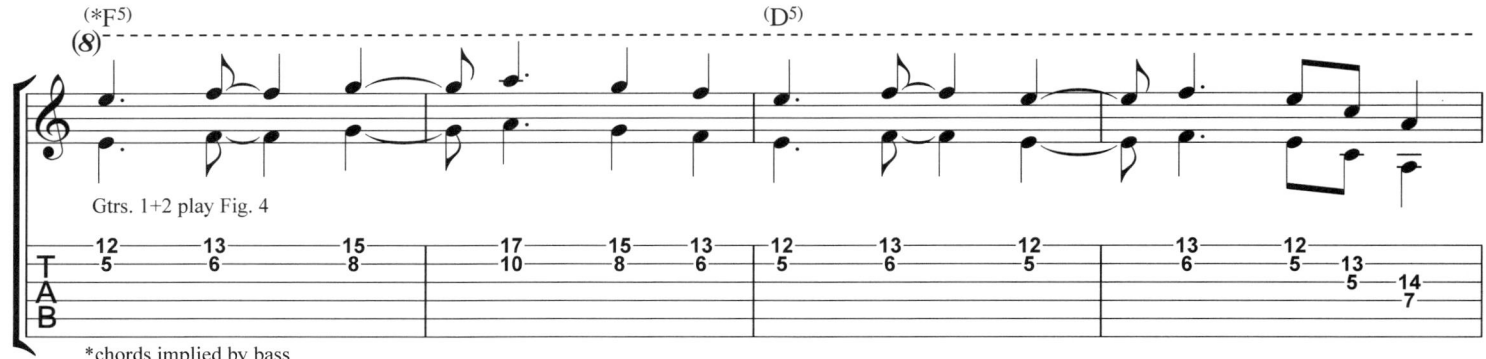
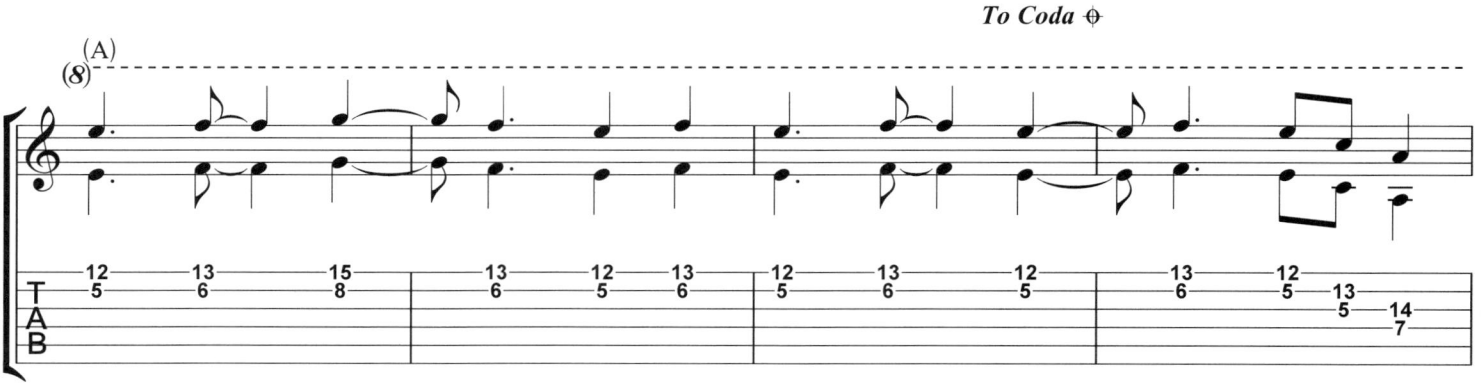
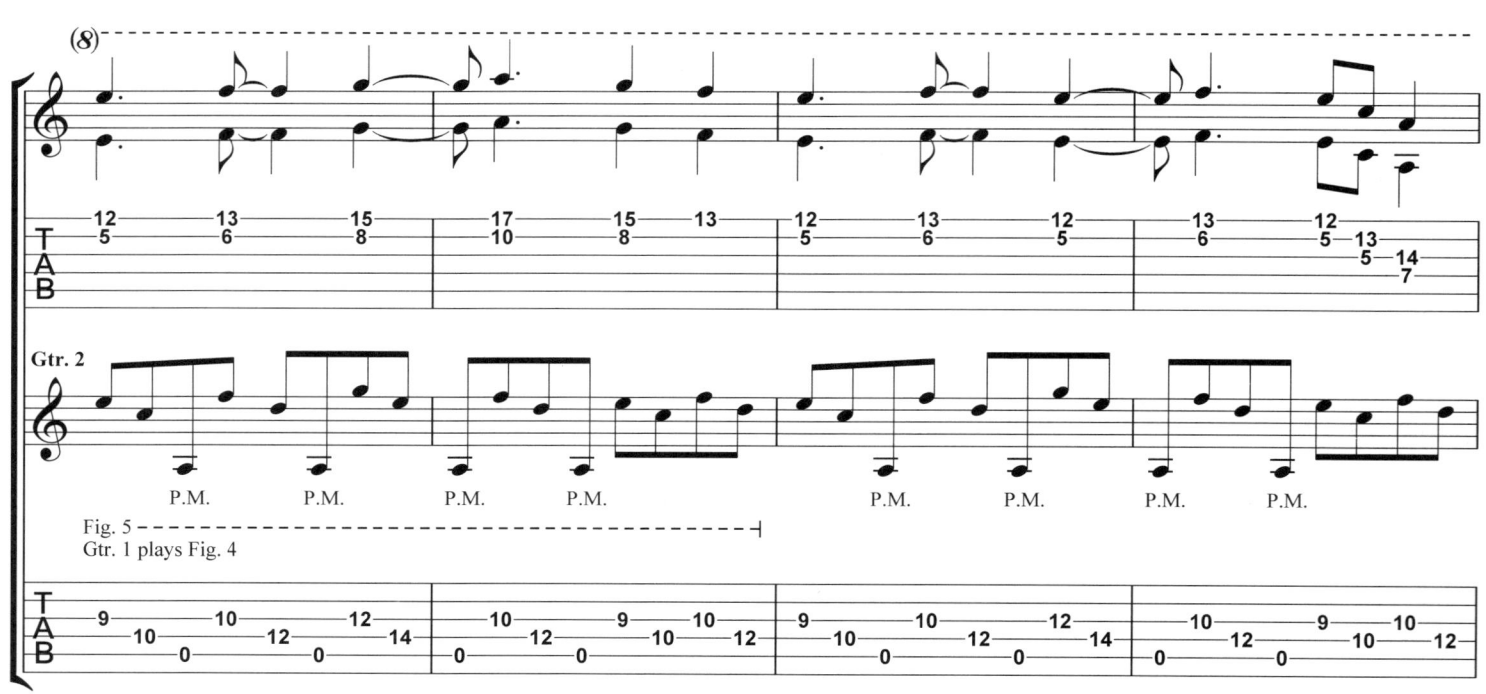

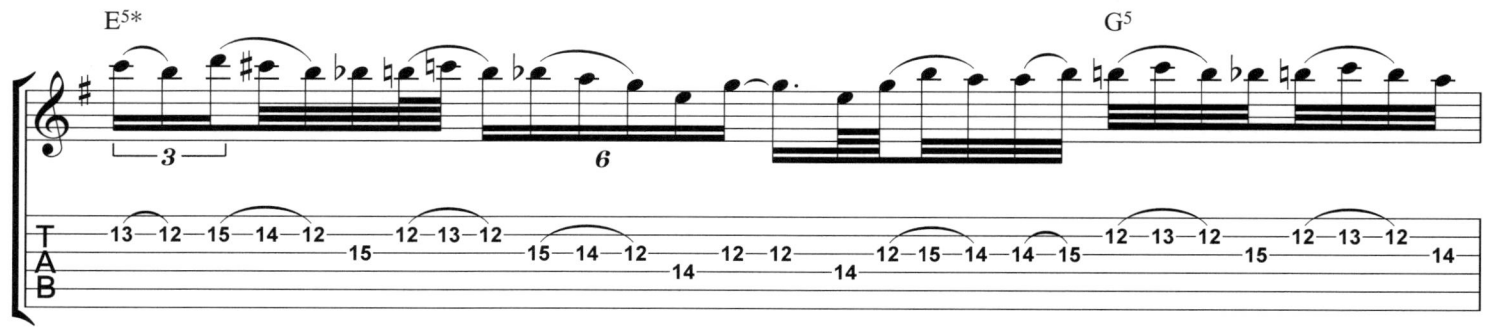
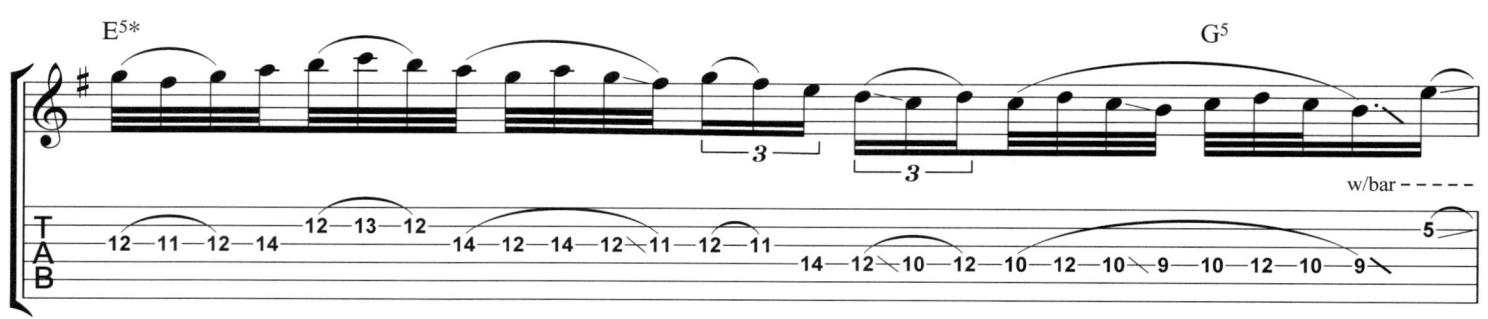
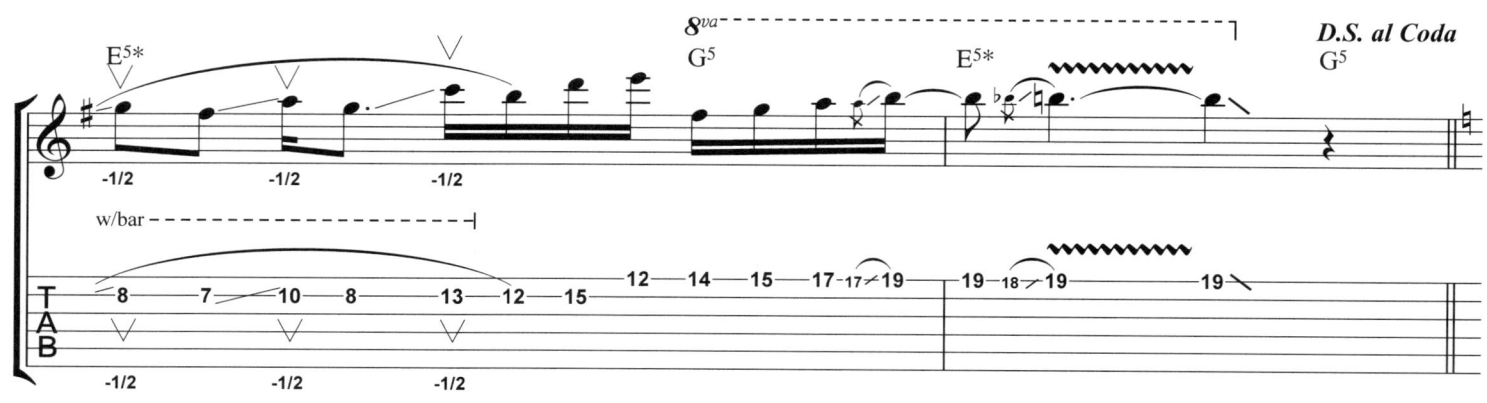
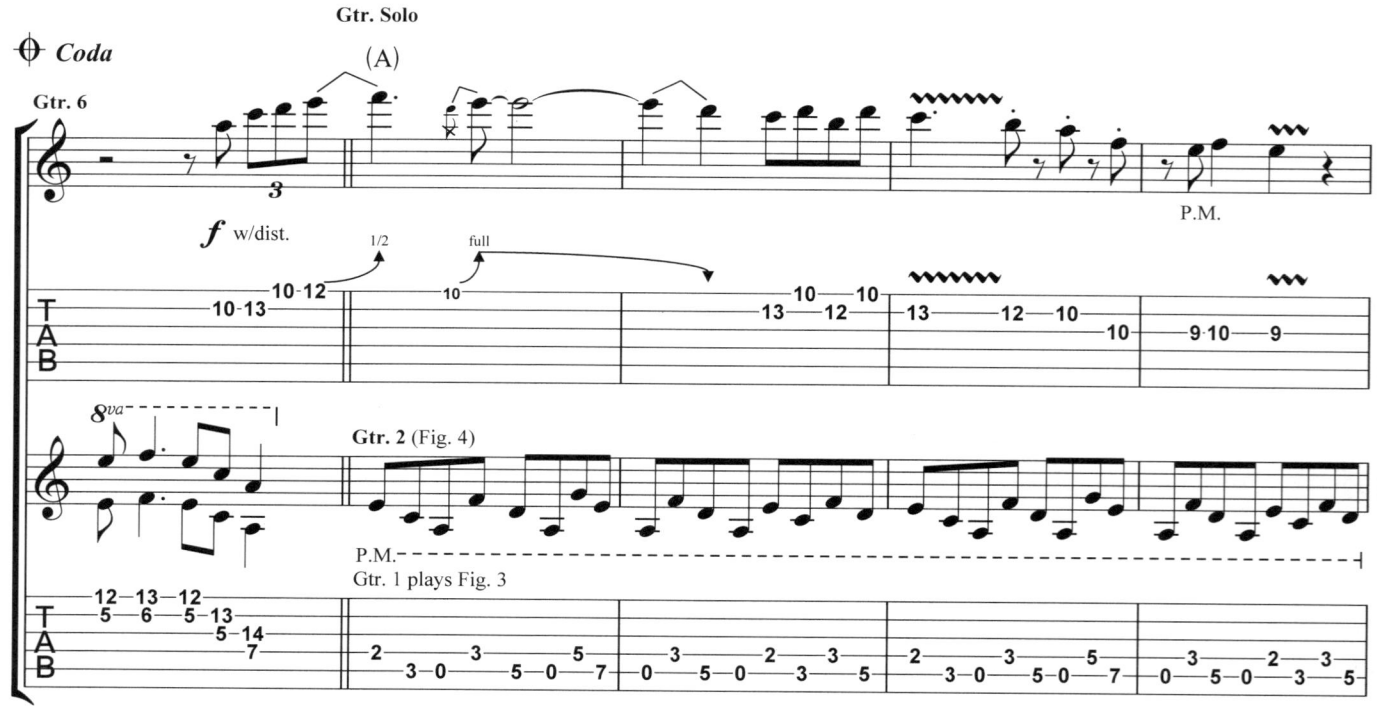

18

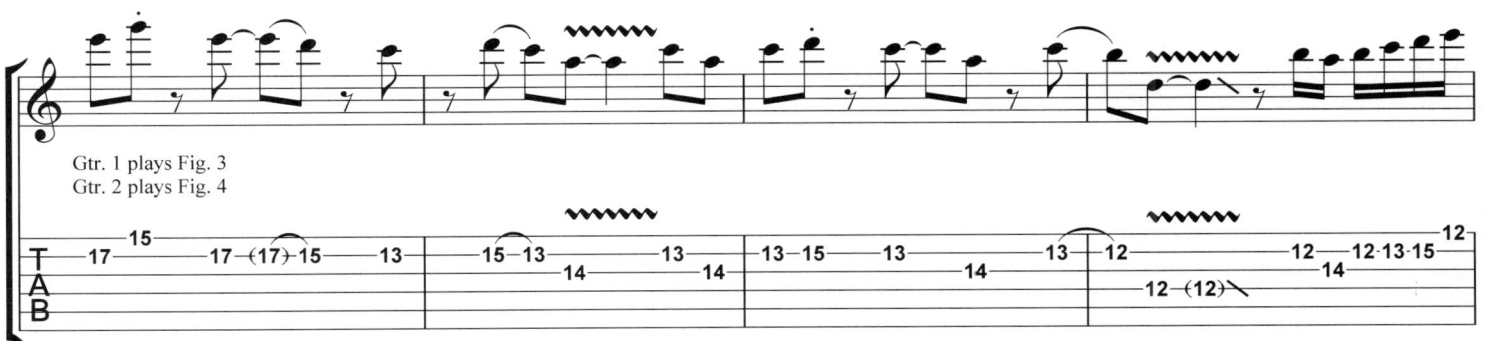

Gtr. 1 plays Fig. 3
Gtr. 2 plays Fig. 4

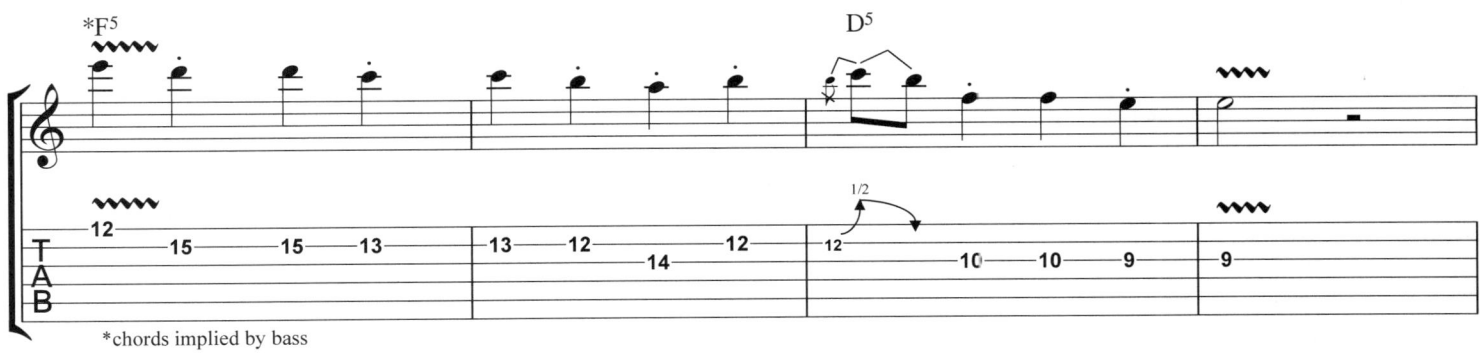

*chords implied by bass

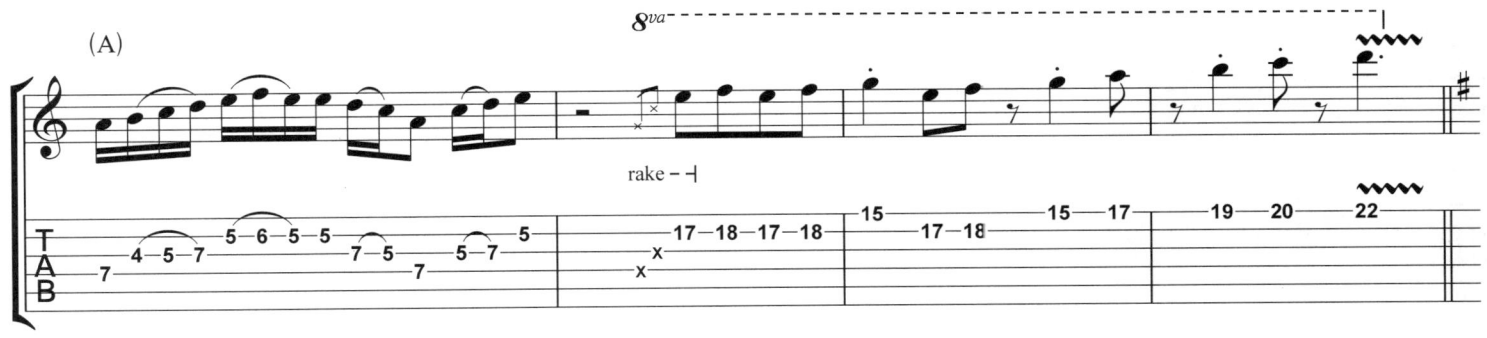

Interlude

Fig. 7...

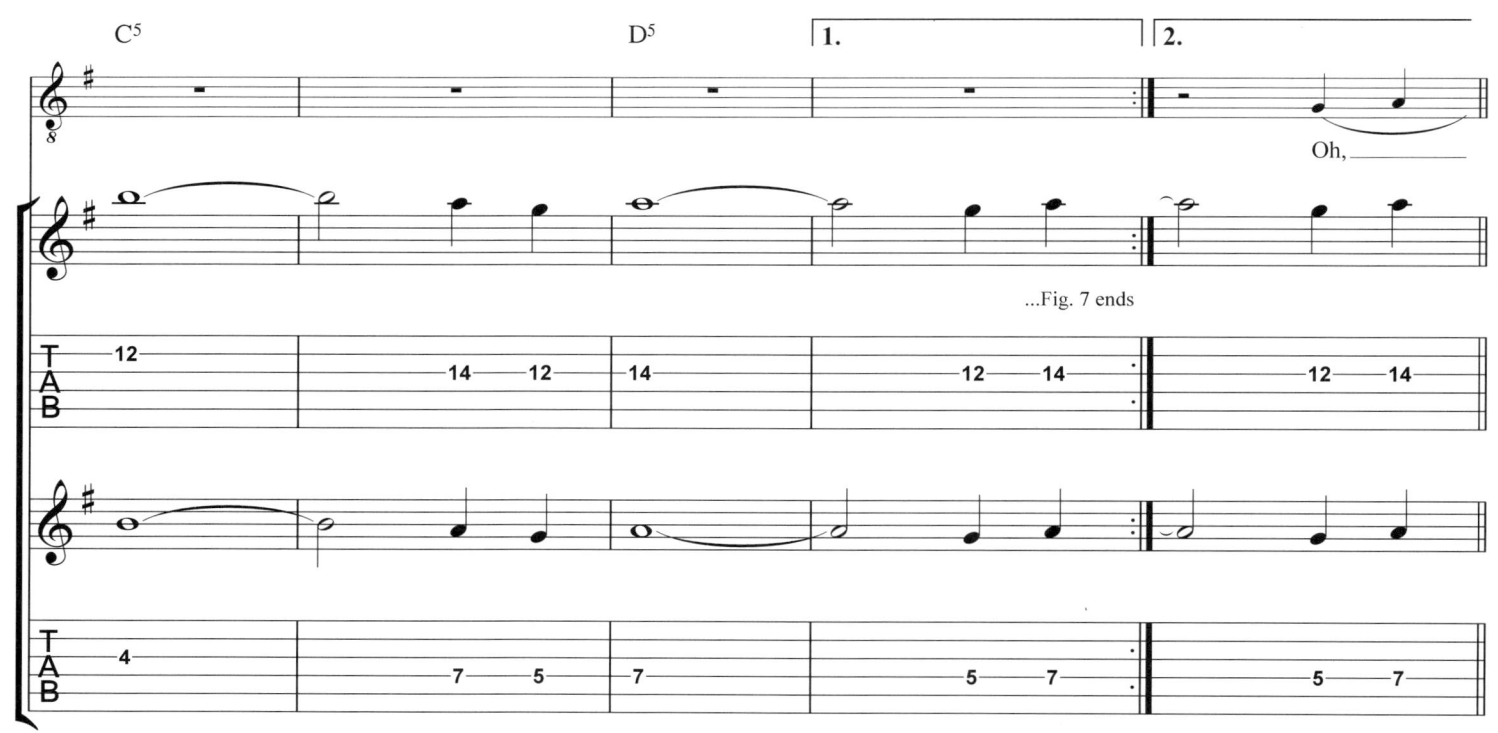

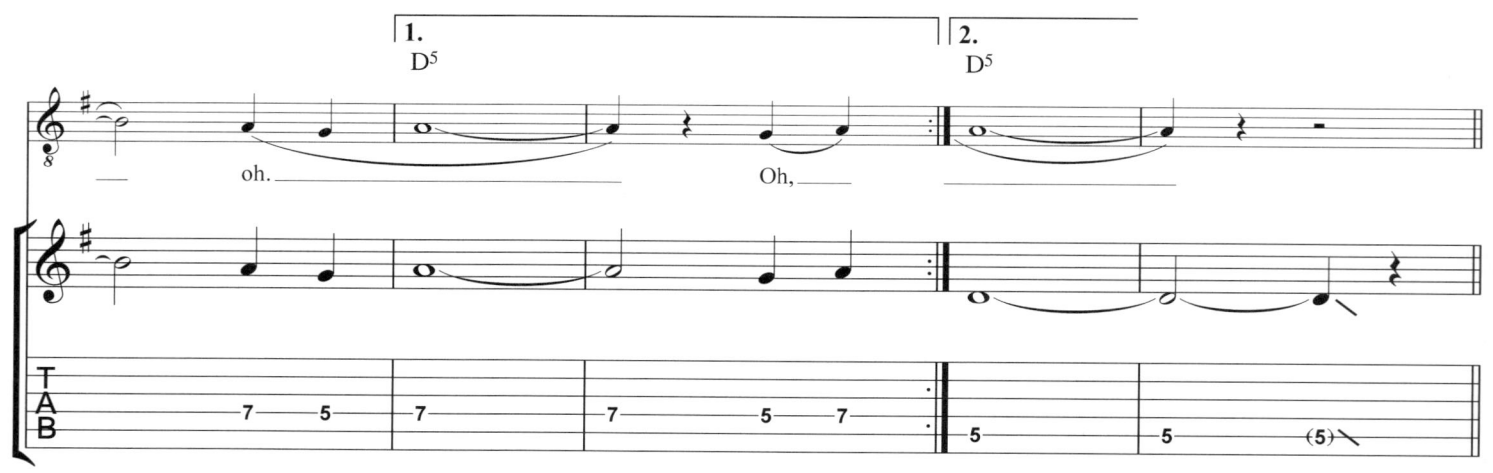

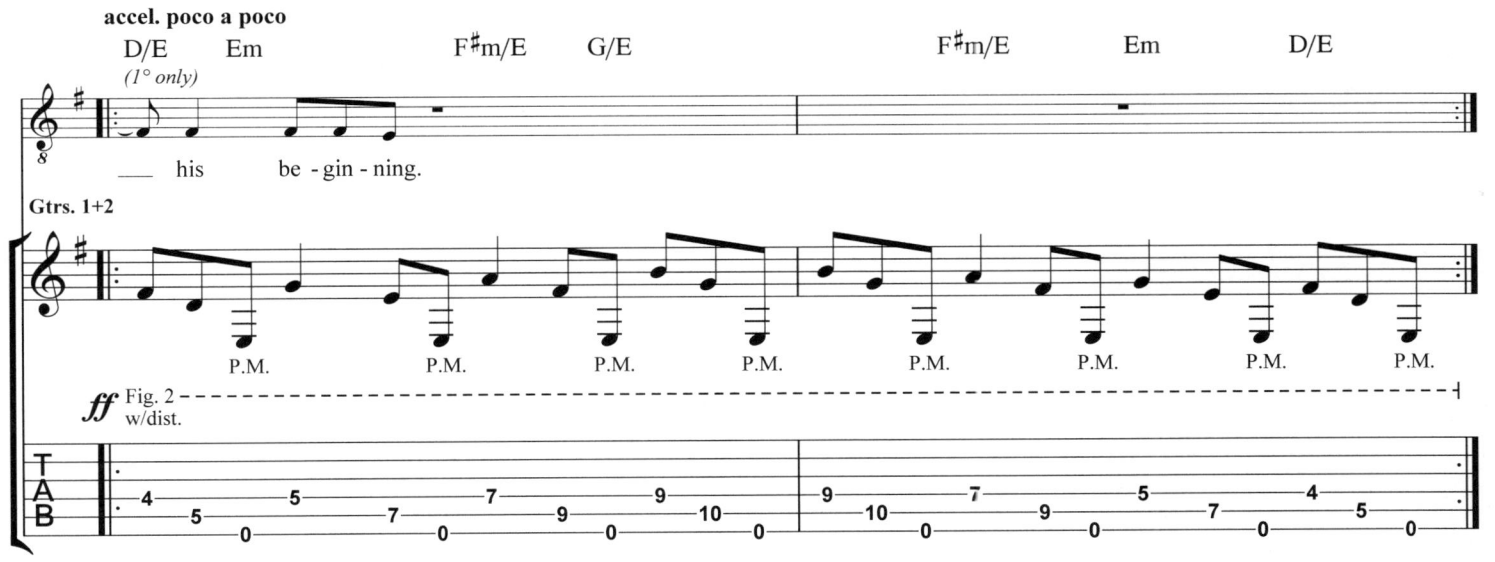
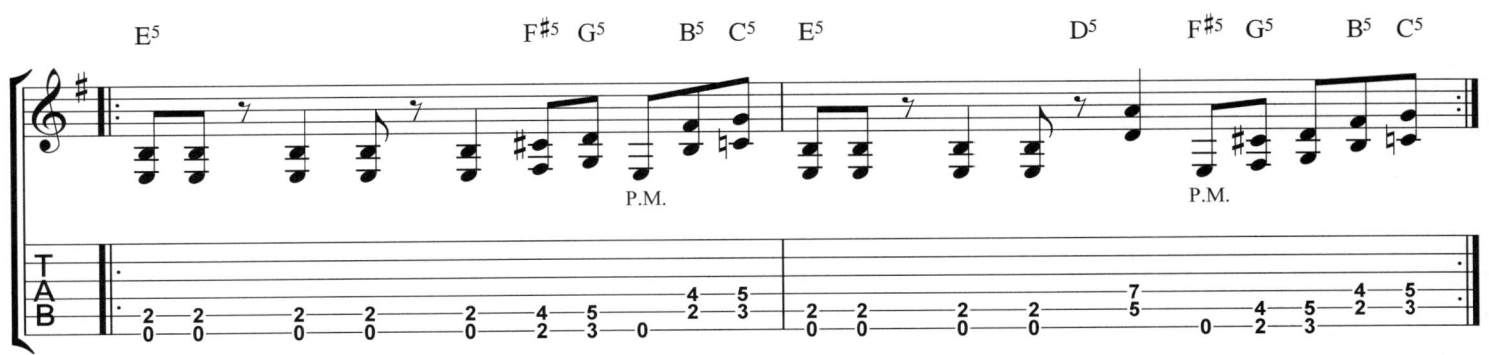
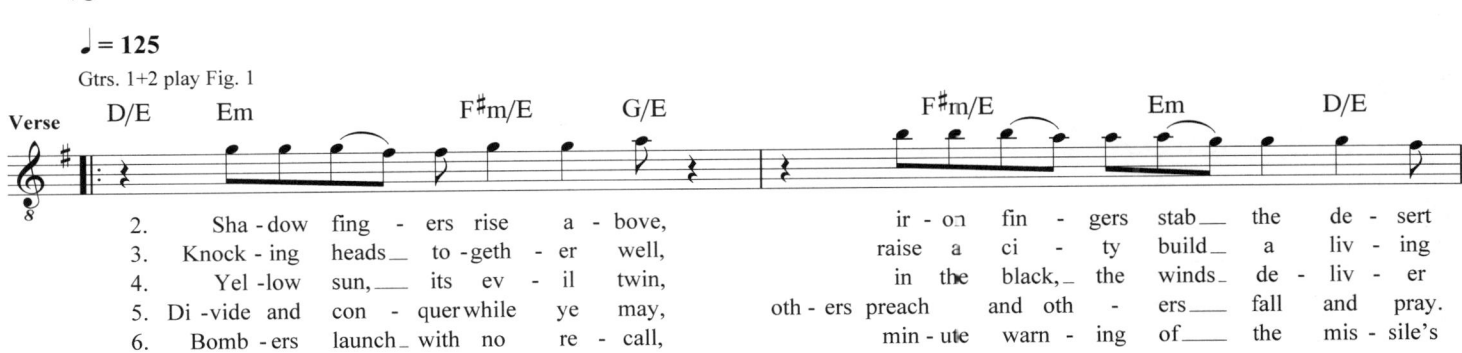
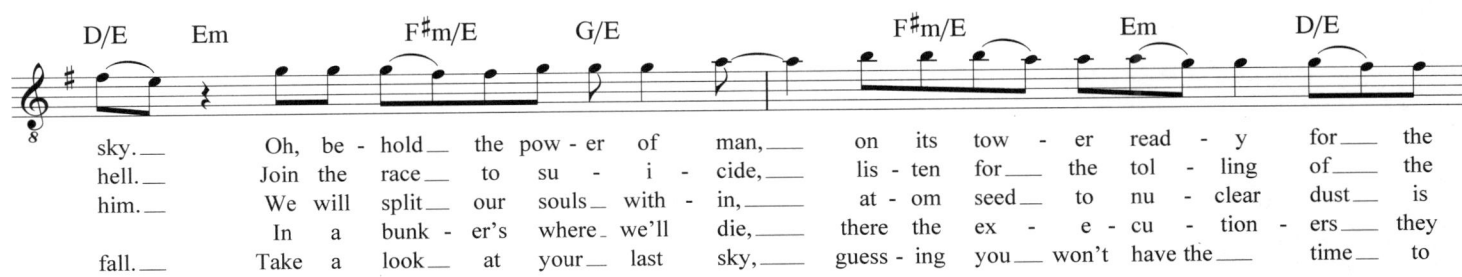

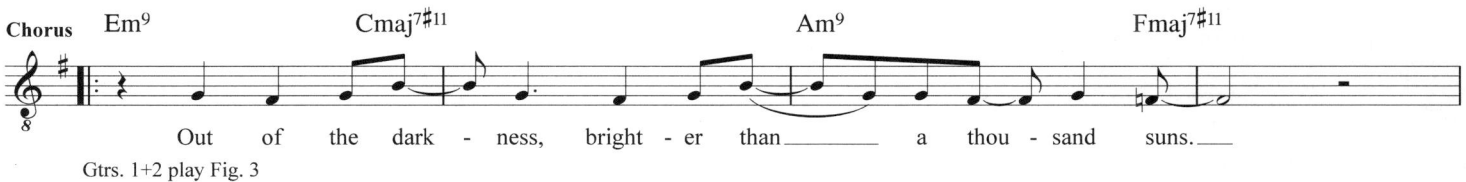
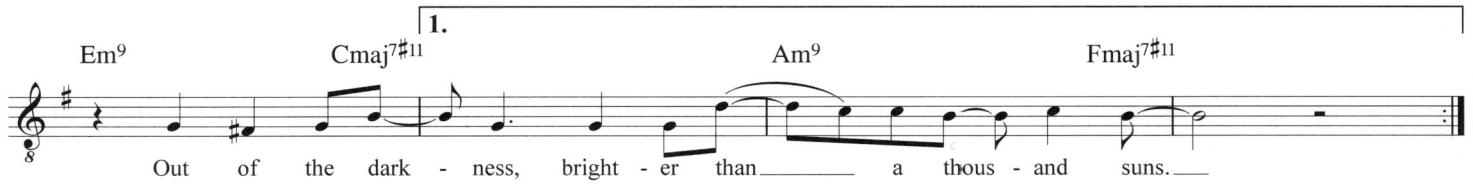
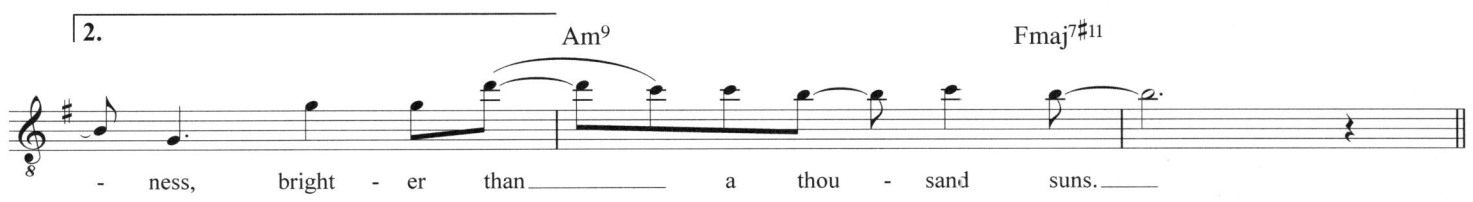
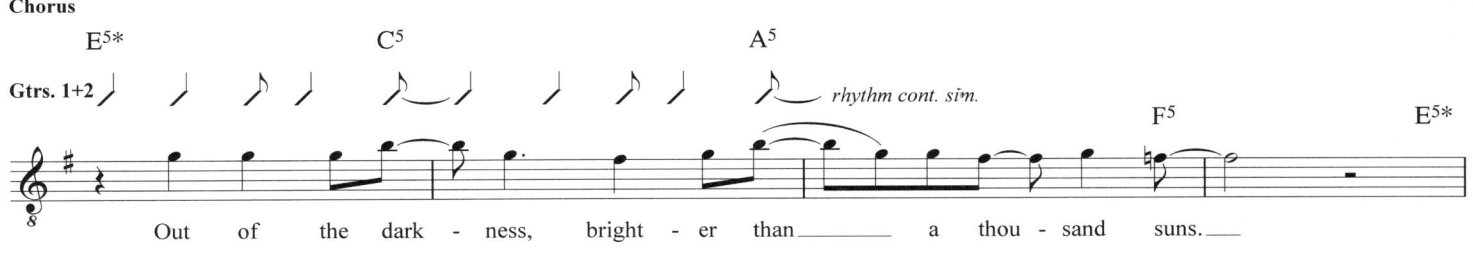
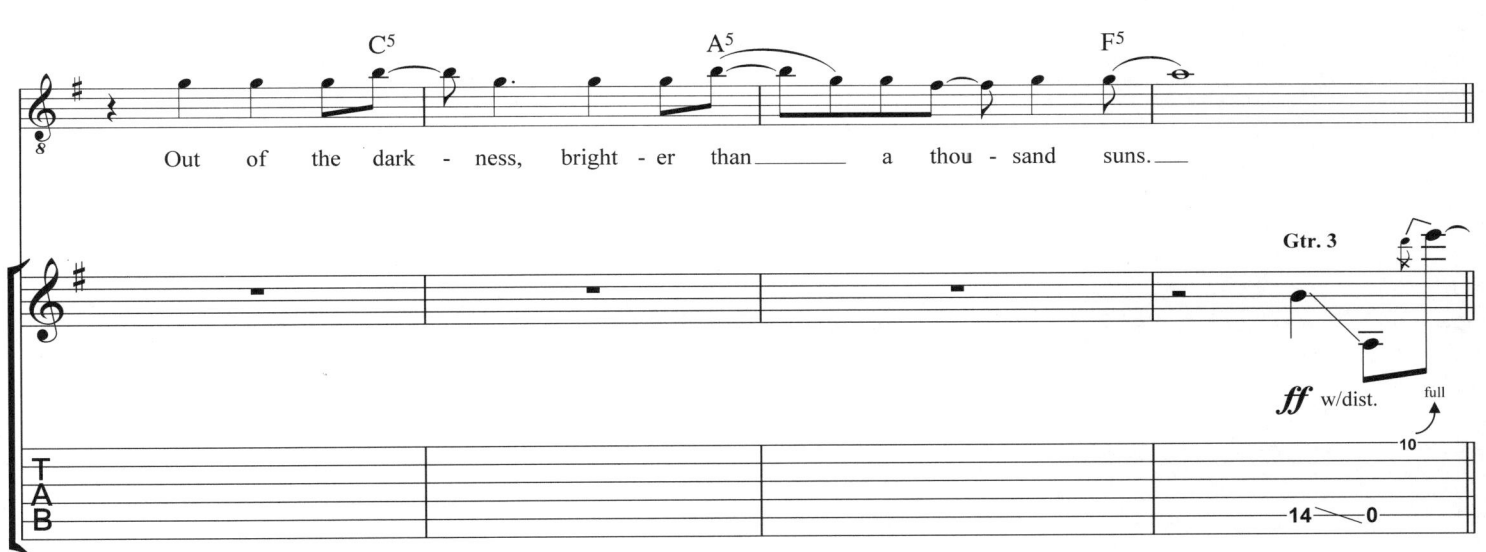

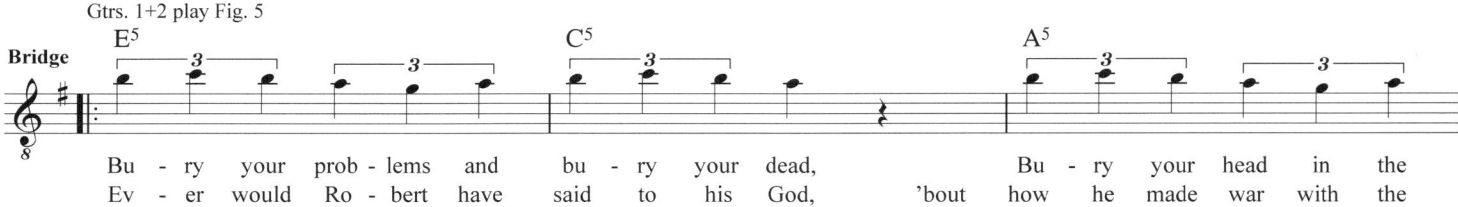
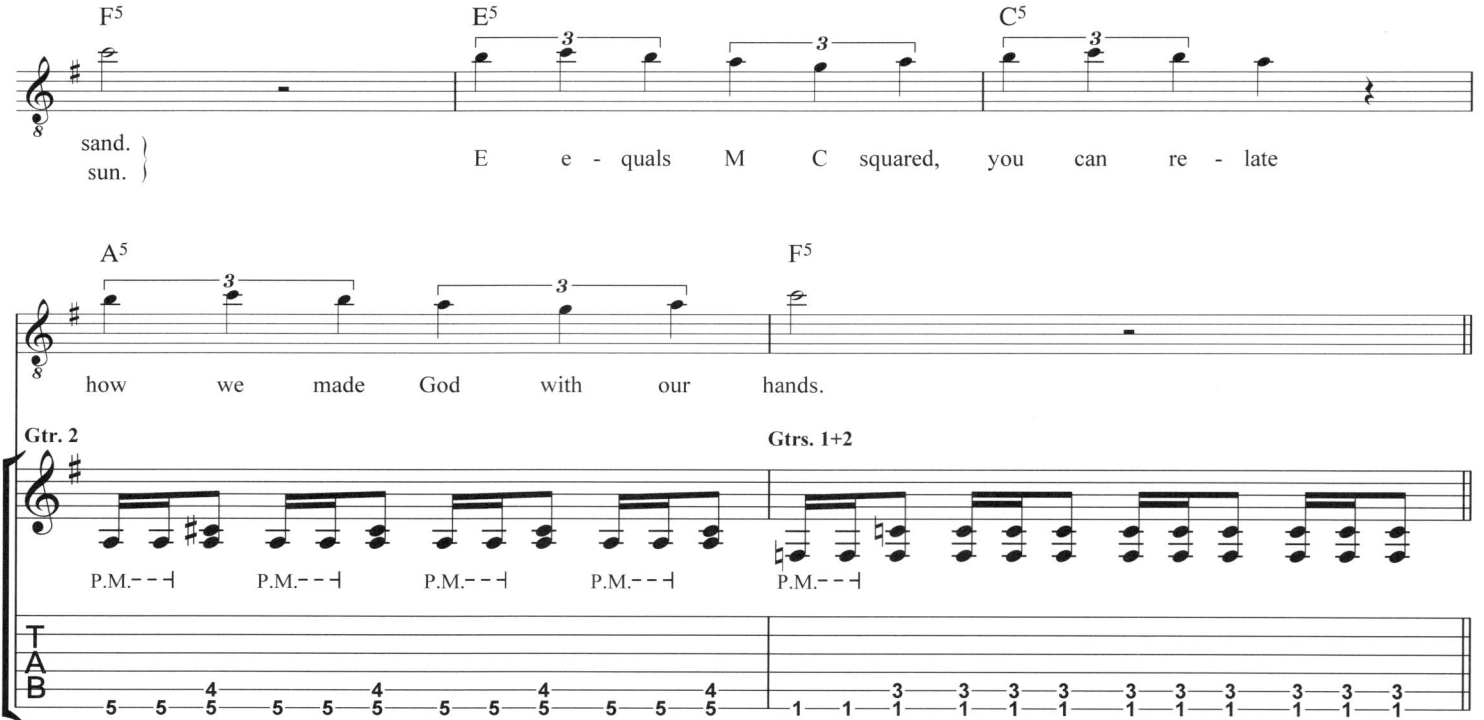
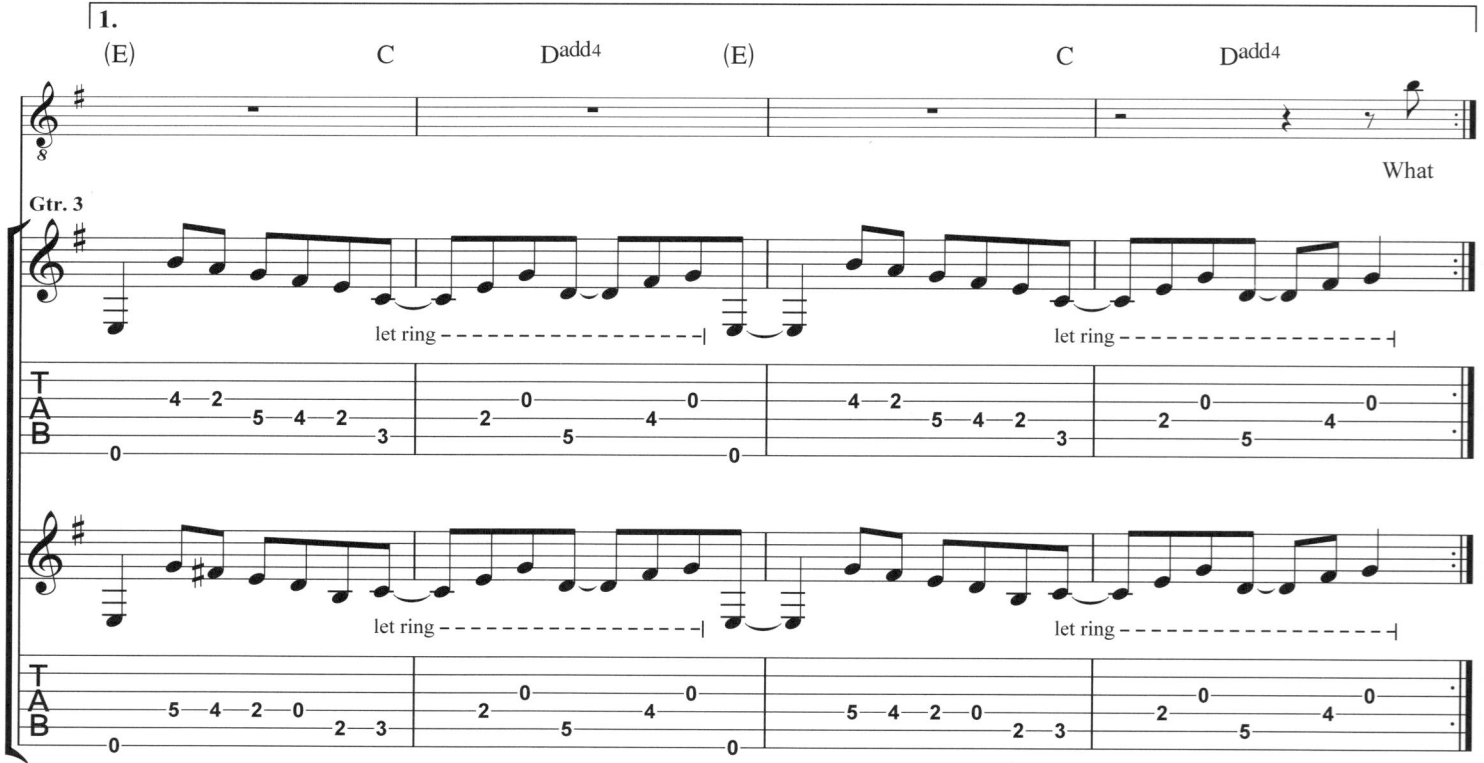

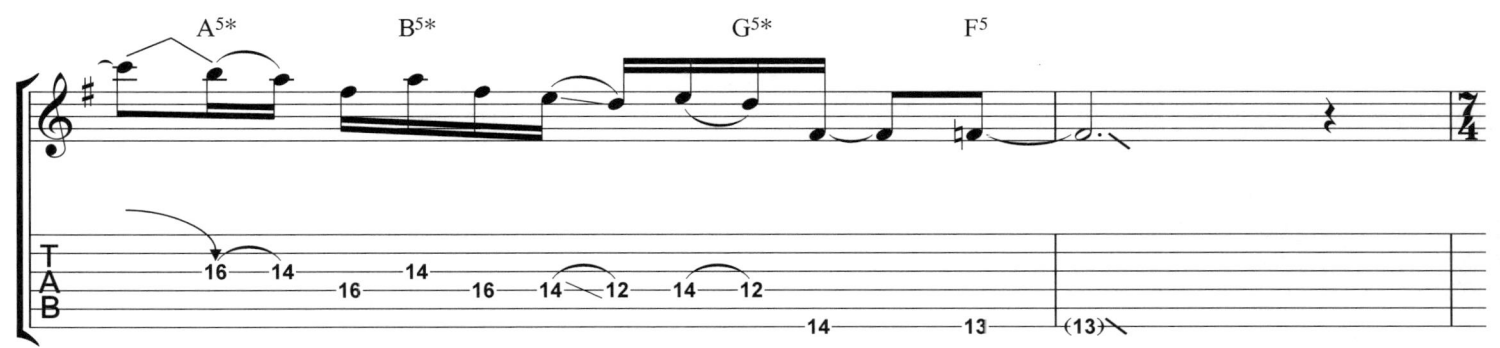
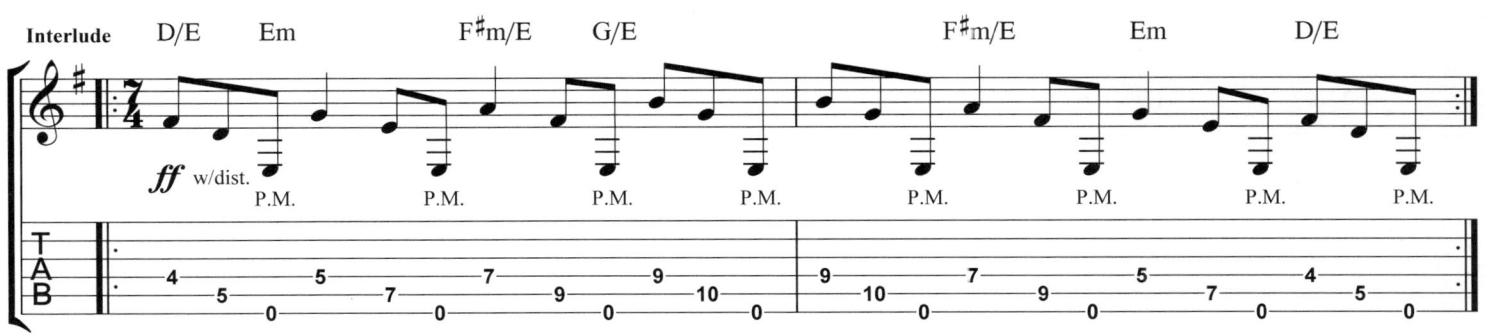
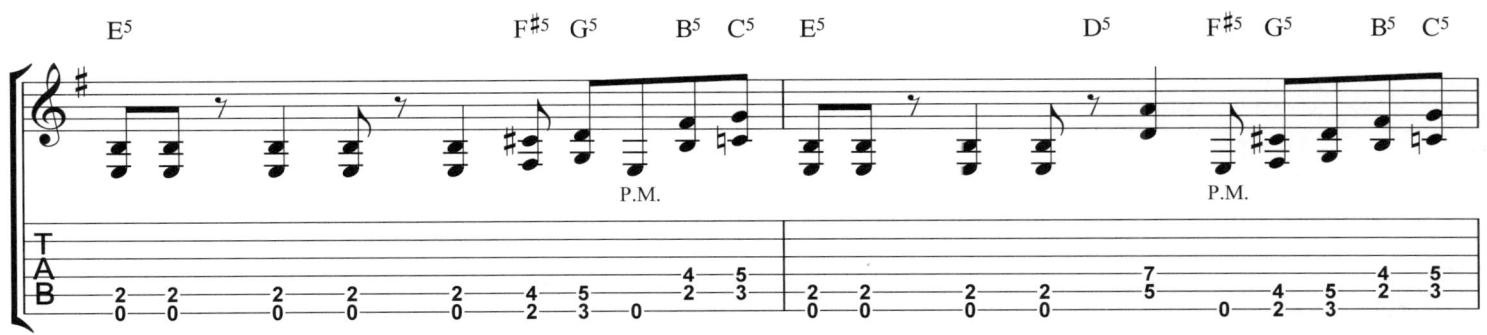
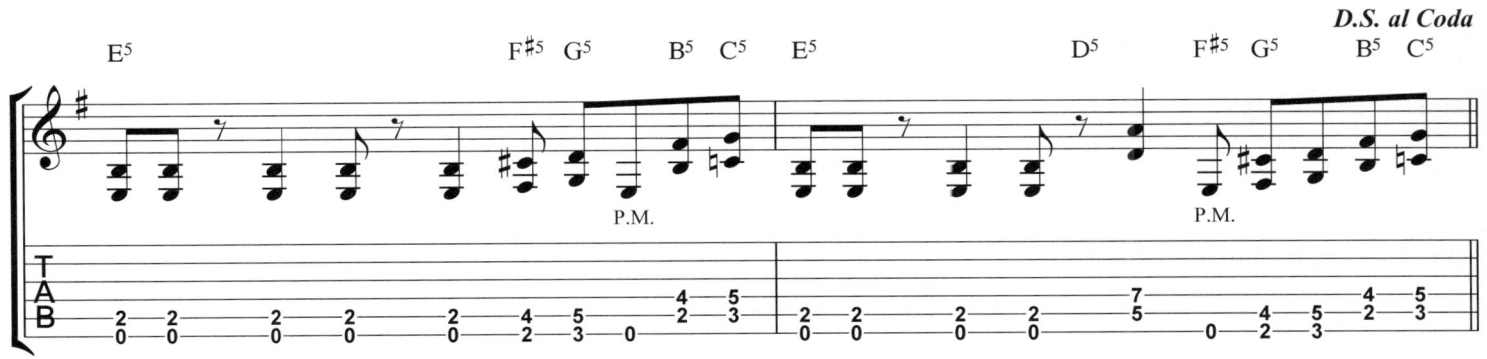

31

THE PILGRIM

Words & Music by Janick Gers & Steve Harris

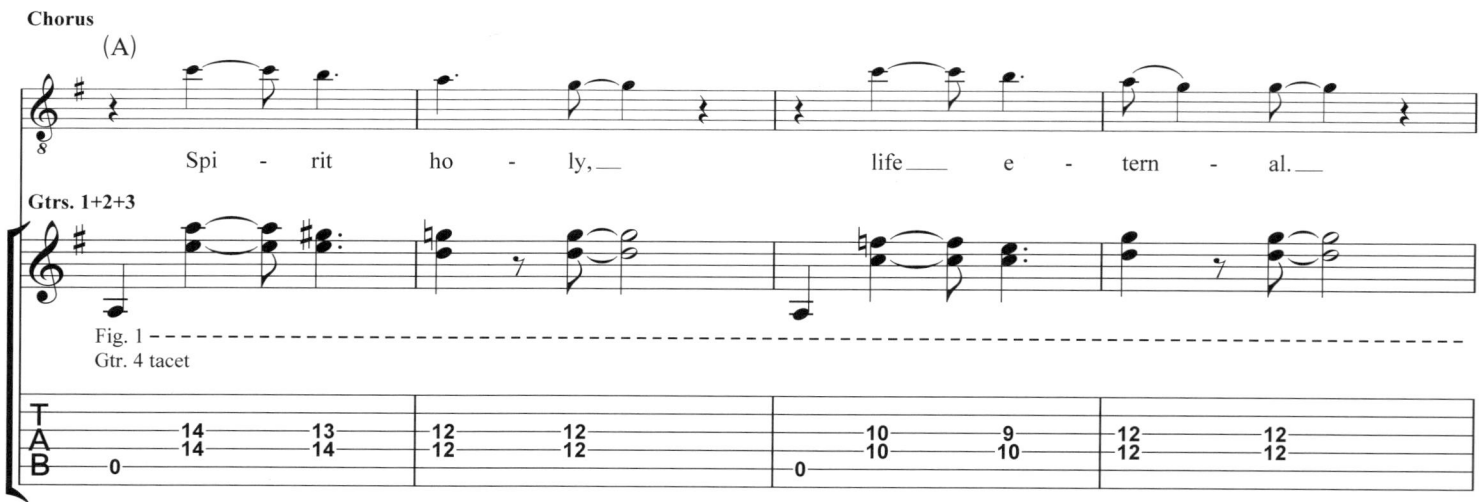
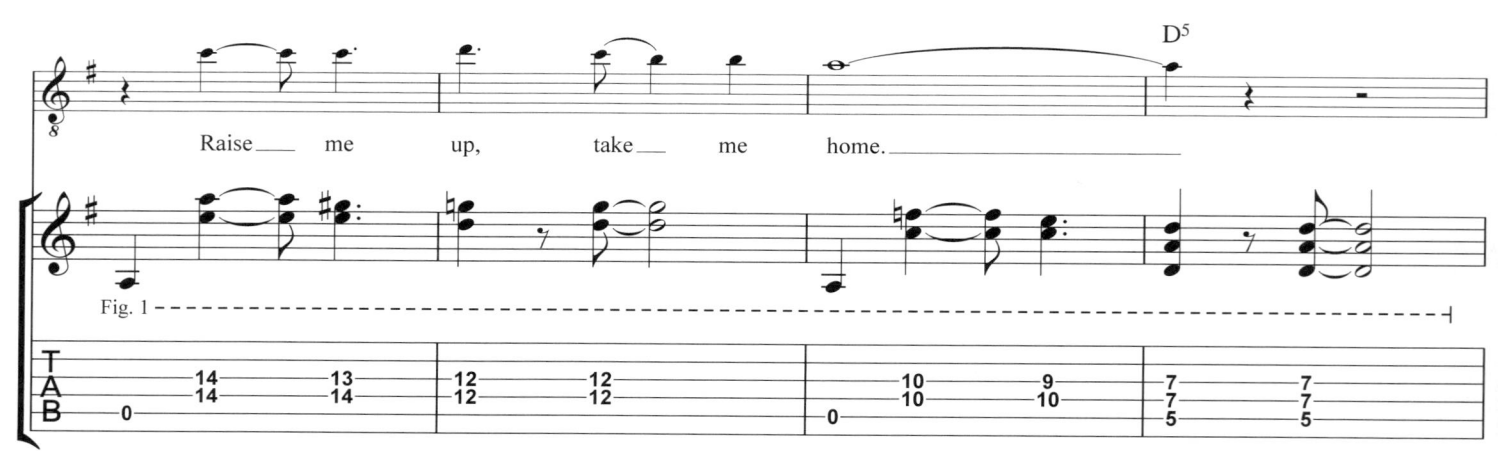

Gtrs. 1+2+3 play Fig. 1
(A)
Pil - grim sun - rise, pa - gan sun - set.
D5
To Coda
On - ward jour - ney be - gun.
Interlude
♩ = 95
E5
F5*
rhythm cont. sim.
Gtr. 3
P.M.
Gtr. 2
Gtr. 1 dbls. ad lib. 8vb
E5
F5
C5
D♭5
C5
1.
D♭5
2.
D♭5
2. To

♩ = 190
Gtr. Solo
Gtr. 5
B5
P.M.
rake
ff w/dist.
full
C5
rhythm cont. sim.
B5/A
1/2
8va

D.S. al Coda
B5/A
B5
C5
D5
(8)
1/2
full
Coda
Gtrs. 1+2+3 play Fig. 1
(A)
Spi - rit ho - ly, life e - tern - al. Raise me
Pil - grim sun - rise, pa - gan sun - set, On - ward
1.
2.
D5
up, take me home.
jour - ney be - gun.
Interlude
♩ = 95
E5
F5
Gtr. 3
rhythm cont. sim.
P.M.
Gtr. 2
Gtr. 1 dbls. ad lib. 8vb
E5
F5

C5
D♭5
C5
D♭5
Outro
Slower
E5 C5 D5 E5 D5 E5 C5
Gtr. 3
Gtrs. 1+2
f w/dist.
Gtr. 4
f w/dist.
rall.
1.
2.
D5 A5
D5 E5 A5

THE LONGEST DAY

**Words & Music by
Steve Harris, Adrian Smith & Bruce Dickinson**

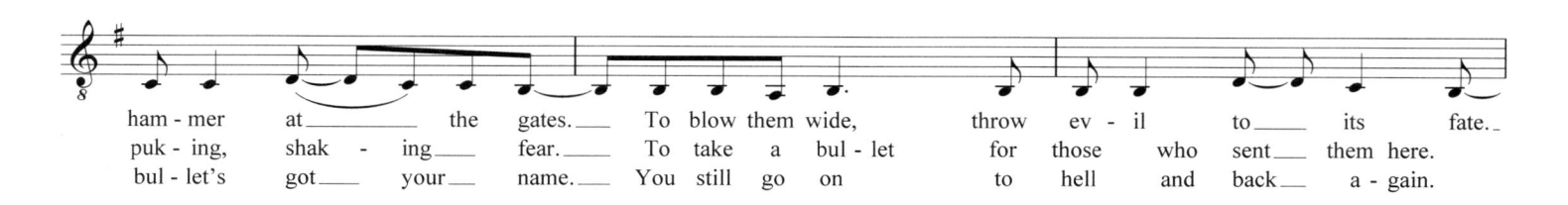

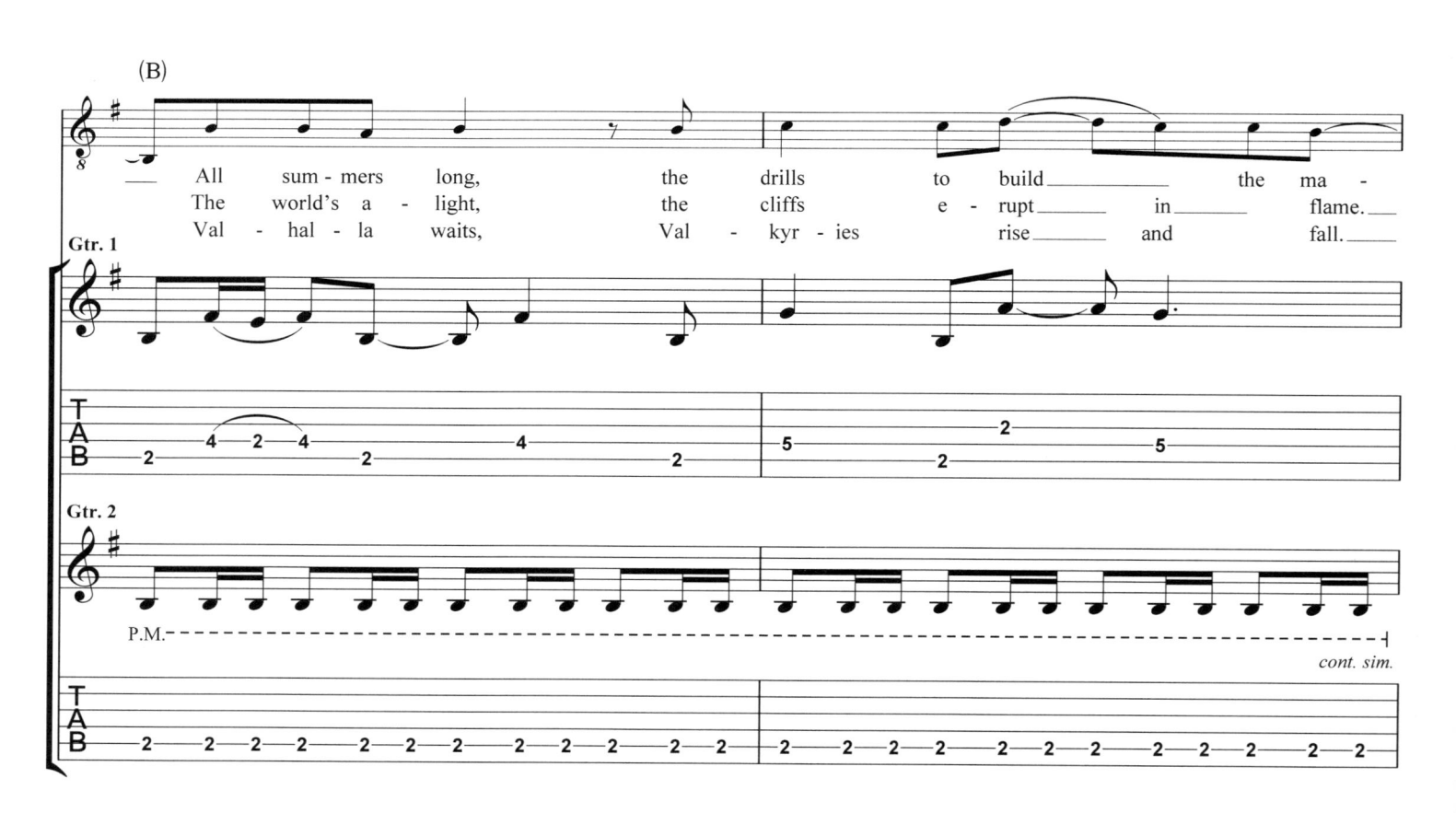

In the ships, gim - let eyes a - wait. A call to arms, to ham - mer at the gates. To blow them wide, throw ev - il to its fate.

The en - e - my coast, dawn - ing grey with scud. These wretch - ed souls, puk - ing, shak - ing fear. To take a bul - let for those who sent them here.

They are re - lieved, the liv - ing wait their turn. Your num - ber's up, the bul - let's got your name. You still go on to hell and back a - gain.

(B)

All sum - mers long, the drills to build the ma-
The world's a - light, the cliffs e - rupt in flame.
Val - hal - la waits, Val - kyr - ies rise and fall.

Gtr. 1

Gtr. 2

P.M. -

cont. sim.

-chine, to turn men from flesh and blood to steel. From pap - er sol - diers to
No es - cape, re - morse - less shrap - nel rains. Drown - ing man, no
The war - ri - or tombs lie op - en for us all. A ghost - ly hand

1.
bo - dies on the beach. From sum - mer sands to ar - ma - ged - don's reach.
chance for a war - ri - or's fate. A chok - ing death,
reach - es through the veil, blood and sand, we
2, 3.
Pre-chorus
rhythm cont. sim.
E5 C5 G5
en - ter hell's gate! Slid - ing we go, on - ly fear
will pre - vail!
ff w/dist. Fig. 2
D5 E5
on our side. To the edge
Fig. 2
Gtr. 1 plays Fig. 1
C5 G5 D5 E5
of the wire, and we rush with the tide. Oh, the wat-
C5 G5 D5 E5
- er is red with the blood of the dead. Oh, but I'm
C5 G5 D5
Gtrs. 1+2
still a - live, pray to God I sur - vive.

Chorus
♩ = 122
Cadd9 Eadd9 Dadd9 Eadd9 Cadd9 Eadd9
How long, on this long - est day, 'til we fin - al - ly make it through?
Gtrs. 1+2
Fig. 3
let ring...
Dadd9 Cadd9 Eadd9 Dadd9 Eadd9
How long, on this long - est day, 'til we
Fig. 3
C5 G/B A5
fin - al - ly make it through?
Fig. 3
Gtrs. 1+2 play Fig. 3
Cadd9 Eadd9 Dadd9 Eadd9 Cadd9 Eadd9
How long, on this long - est day, 'til we fin - al - ly make it through?
To Coda
Dadd9 Cadd9 Eadd9 Dadd9 Eadd9 C5 G/B
How long, on this long - est day, 'til we fin - al - ly make it through?

1.
A5
Asus4
2.
A5
Gtrs 1+2
T
A
B
♪ = 190
E5 G5* F♯5 D5 E5 G5 F♯5 E5 G5* F♯5 D5
E5 G5* F♯5 D5 E5 G5 F♯5 E5 G5* F♯5 C5
(E)
(F)
P.M.
P.M.
(E)
(F)
P.M.
P.M.

(B)
(C)
P.M.
P.M.
1.
2.
(B)
(C)
(C)
Gtr. 3
ff w/dist.
P.M.
P.M.
P.M.
cont. in slashes
Gtr. Solo
Eadd9
Badd9
Gadd9
Aadd9
Eadd9
Badd9
Gtrs. 1+2
rhythm cont. sim.
8va
full
full
full
Gadd9
Aadd9
Eadd9
Badd9

Gadd9
Aadd9
Eadd9
8va
Badd9
Gadd9
Aadd9
Gtr. 4
Gtr. 5
Gtr. 6

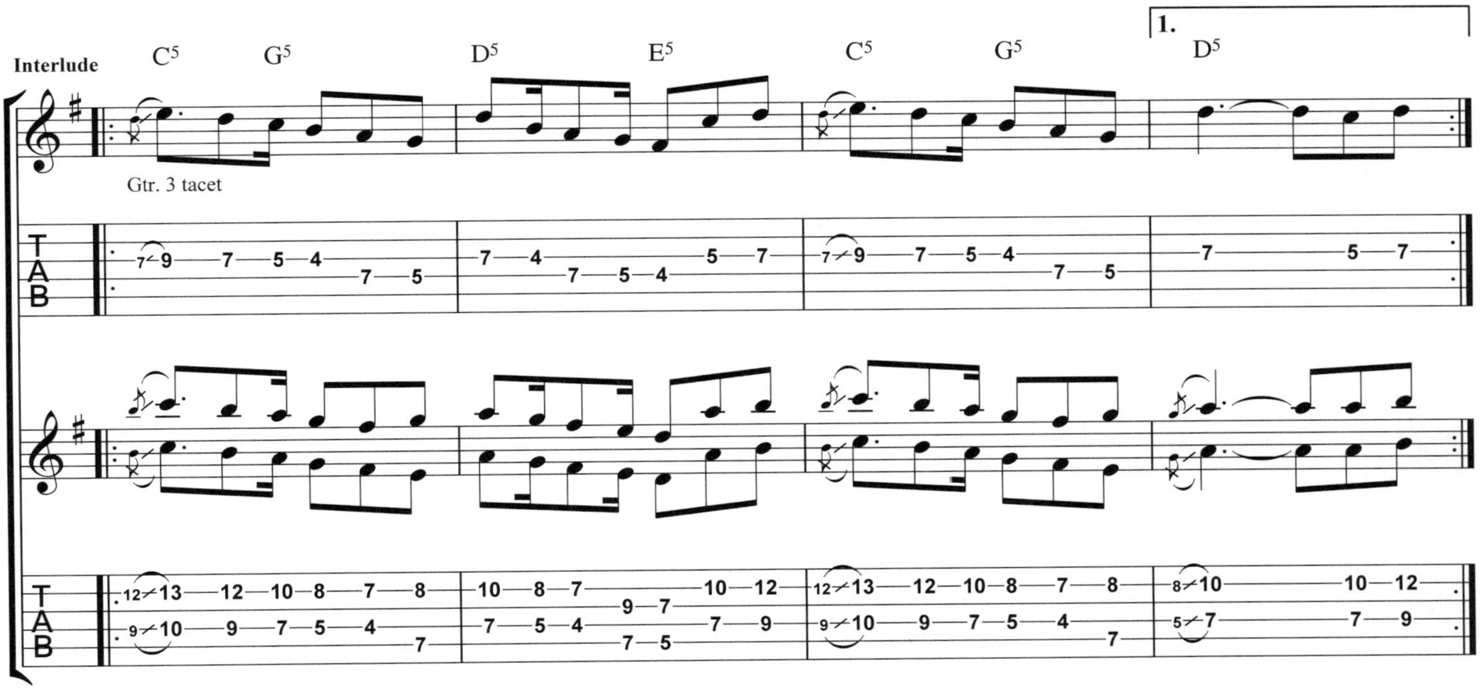
Interlude
C5
G5
D5
E5
C5
G5
1.
D5
Gtr. 3 tacet

2.
A5
Gtrs. 1+2
E5
Gtrs 4+5+6 tacet
Gtrs. 1+2
1.
P.M.
Fig. 5
Fig. 4
2.
C5
G5
D5
E5
rhythm cont. sim.
Gtr. 4
Gtrs. 1+2 play Fig. 4
Gtr. 3 plays Fig. 5
Gtr. 3 tacet
Gtr. 5
Gtr. 6

1.
2, 3.
C5 G5 D5 D5
Gtr. 3 8va
cont. sim.
cont. sim.
Gtr. Solo
C5 G5 D5 E5 C5 G5
full
D5 C5 G5 D5 E5
C5 G5 D5
D.S. al Coda

Coda
A5
Asus4
Gtr. 1
(E)
mf
let ring...
w/slight dist.
Gtr. 2
mf
P.M.
w/dist.+flanging
cont. sim.
rall.

OUT OF THE SHADOWS

Words & Music by
Steve Harris & Bruce Dickinson

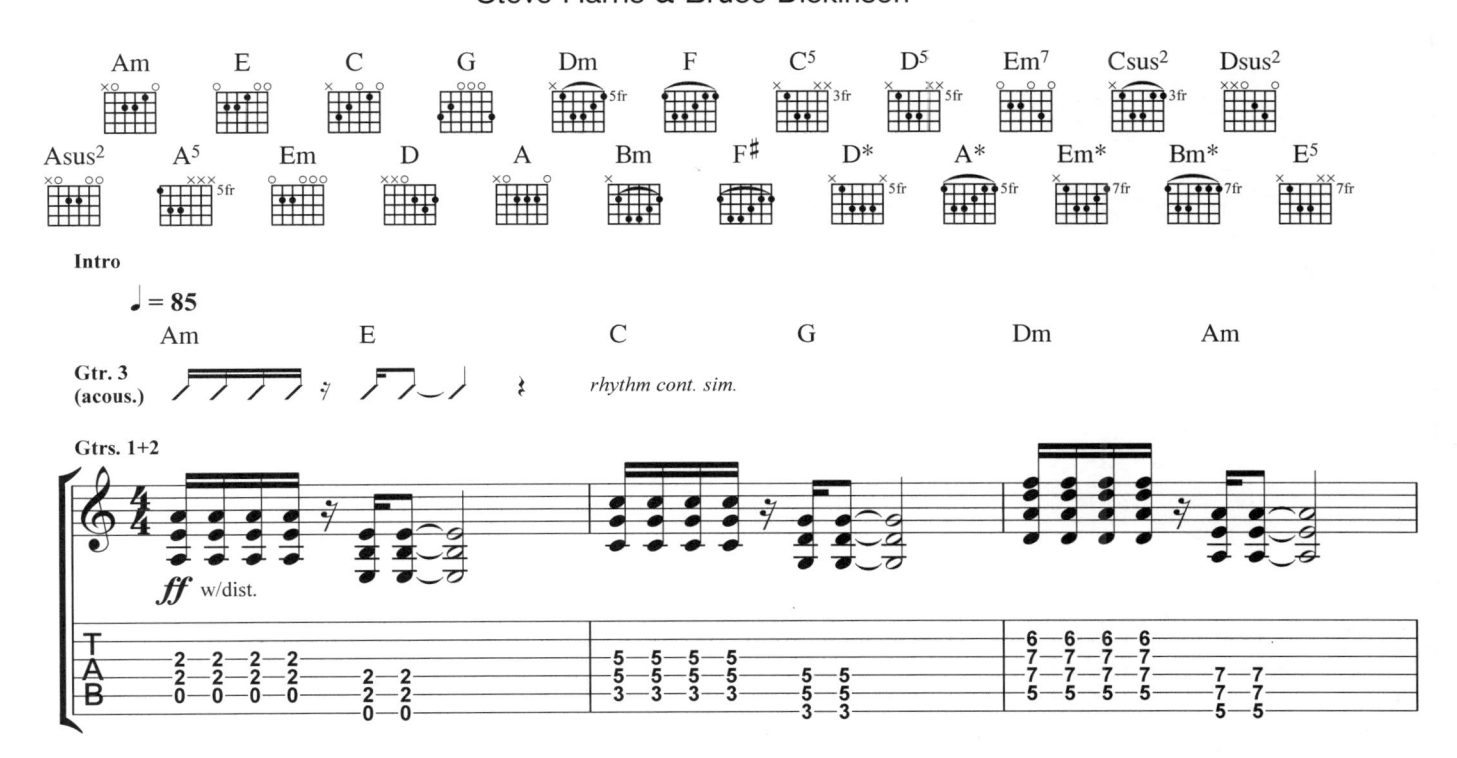

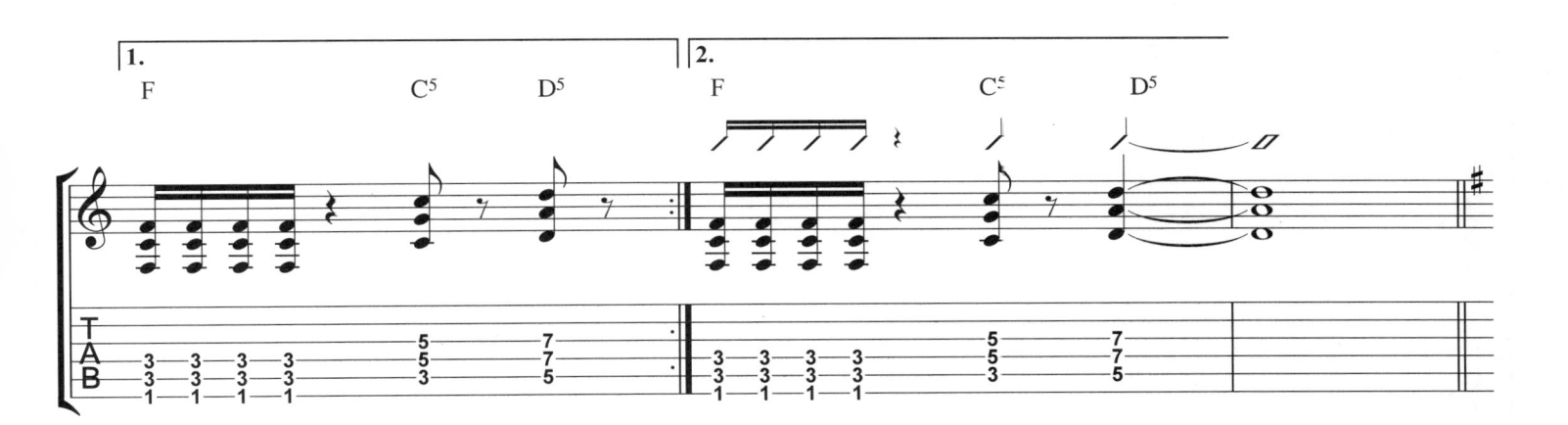

Em7 Csus2 Dsus2 Asus2
Gtr. 4
f w/dist.
full 1/2 full
Verse
Gtrs. 1+2 play Fig. 1
Em7 Csus2 Em7 Csus2 Em7 Csus2
1. Hold a ha - lo round the world, gold - en is the day. Princ - es of the un - i - verse, your
2. Dust-y dreams in fad - ing day-light, flick-er on the walls. No-thing new, your life's a - drift, what
Dsus2 Asus2 Em7 Csus2
bur - den is the way. So there is no bet - ter time, who
pur - pose to it all? Eyes are closed and death is call - ing,
Gtr. 4 (2° only)
1/2
Em7 Csus2 Em7 Csus2
will be born to - day? A gyp - sy child at day - break, a
reach-ing out his hand. Call up - on the star - light, to sur -
Gtr. 4 (2° only)
rake
1/2

king for a day.
-round you.

Chorus

Out of the sha-dow, and in to the sun.

Dreams of the past, as the old ways are done.

Oh, there is beau-ty, and sure-ly there is pain. But we must en-dure it to

D
A
live a - gain.
Gtr. 4
full
Gtr. 5
f w/dist.+echo
Gtrs. 1+2
Em7
Csus2
Gtr. Solo
Gtrs. 1+2 play Fig. 1
Gtrs. 3+4 tacet
Dsus2
Asus2
rake
P.M.
D.S. al Coda

Coda
D
A
live a - gain.
Gtr 4
P.M.
1/4
full
full
Gtrs 1+2
Interlude
♩ = 93
Bm
F♯
D*
A*
Gtr. 3 (acous.)
Fig. 3
Gtr 6 (elec.) dbls. w/dist.
Gtrs. 1+2+4 tacet
Em*
Bm*
G
D5
E5
Gtrs. 1+2
Bm
F♯
D*
A*
Fig. 4
Gtr. 3 plays Fig. 3

Em* Bm* G D5 E5
Interlude
Gtr. 4
Bm F♯ D* A* Em* Bm*
Gtrs. 1+2 play Fig. 4
G D5 E5 C5 D5
Gtrs. 1+2+3
D.S. al Coda
P.M.
Coda
Gtrs. 1+2 play Fig. 2
Gtr. 4 plays ad lib.
D A Em C D A
live a - gain. Out of the sha - dow, and in to the sun.
Em C D A Em C
Dreams of the past, as the old ways are done. Oh, there is beau - ty, and
D A Em C
sure - ly there is pain. But we must en - dure it to

live a - gain.

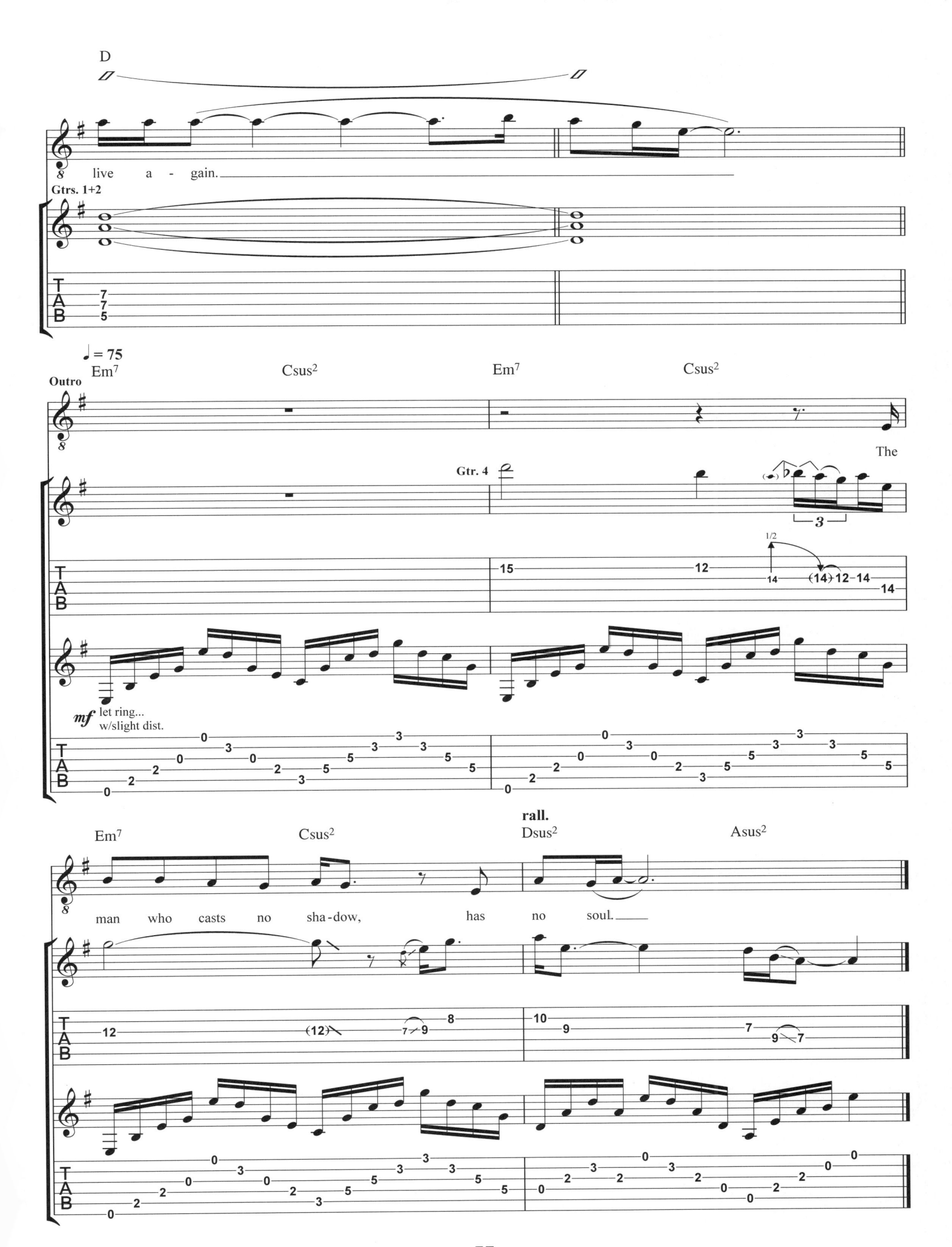

Outro — ♩ = 75

man who casts no sha-dow, has no soul.

57

THE REINCARNATION OF BENJAMIN BREEG

**Words & Music by
Steve Harris & David Murray**

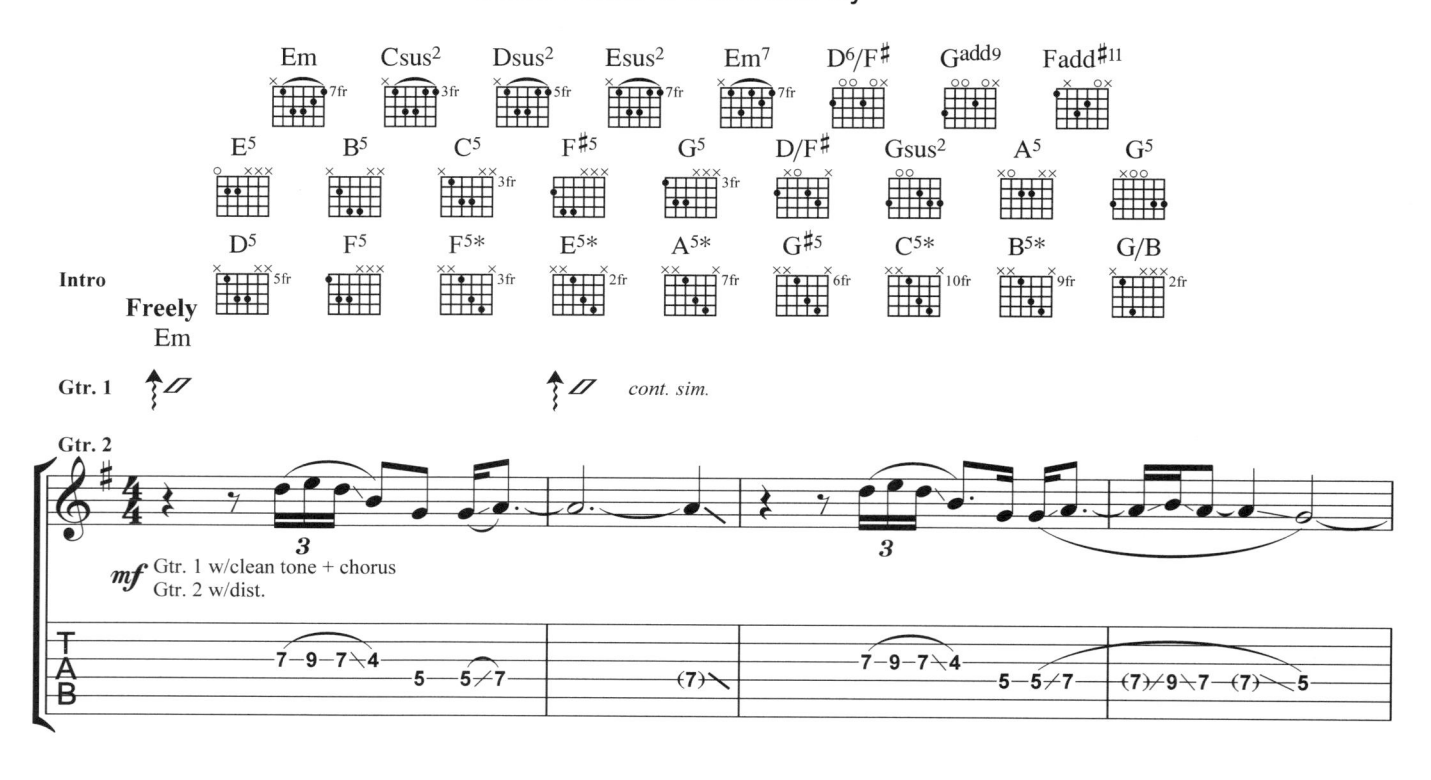

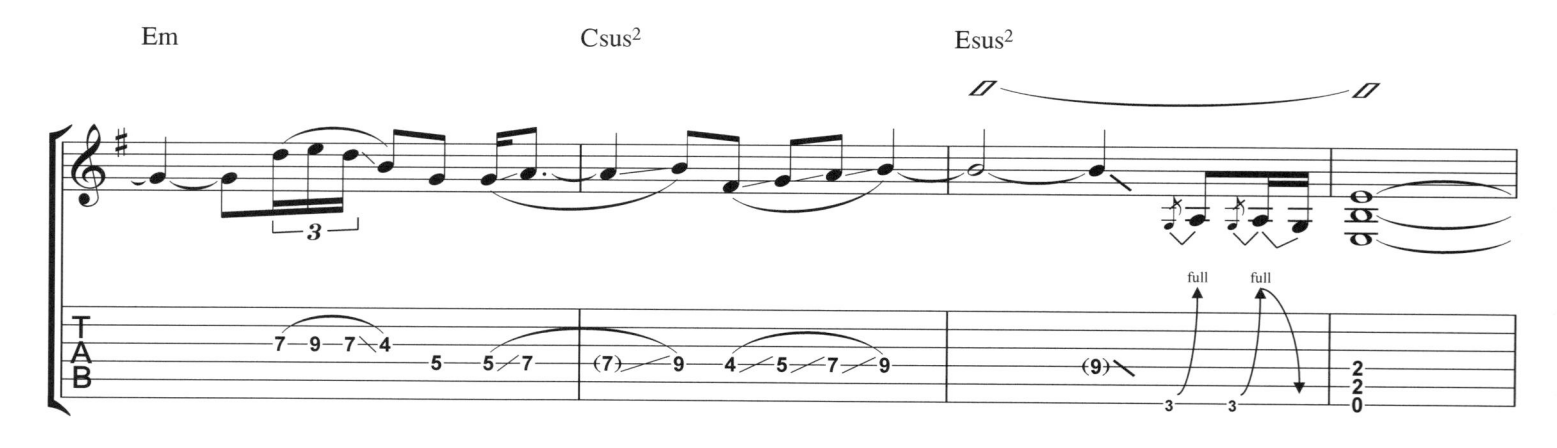

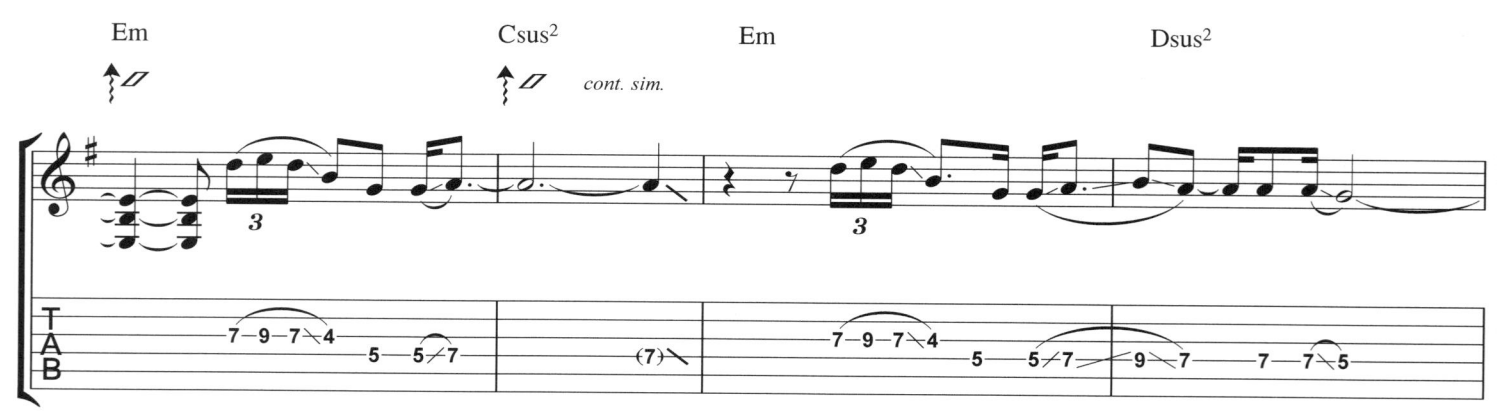

© Copyright 2006 Iron Maiden Publishing (Overseas) Limited.
BMG Music Publishing Limited.
All Rights Reserved. International Copyright Secured.

Em
Csus
Esus2
♩ = 110
1. Let me
rake
Verse
Em7
(E5)
tell you 'bout my life, let me tell you 'bout my dreams. Let me
Gtr. 3
mf
Gtr. 3 let ring w/clean tone
Gtrs 1+2 tacet
tell you 'bout the things that hap - pen, al - ways real to me. Let me
D6/F#
Gadd9
Fadd#11
tell you of my hope, of my need to reach the sky. Let me

(E5)
take you on an awkward journey, let me tell you why.
D6/F#
Gadd9
Fadd#11
(E5)
Let me tell you why.
Gtrs. 3+4
Gtr. 4
Harm.
Gtr. 3 plays Fig. 1

Harm.
Gtrs. 5+6
ff w/dist.
E5 B5 C5 F♯5 G5 F♯5 E5 E5 B5 C5 F♯5 G5 F♯5 E5
P.M.
Gtrs. 3+4 tacet
P.M.
cont. in slashes
Verse
E5 D/F♯ Gsus2 A5
Gtrs. 5+6
Why should these cur - ses be laid up - on me? I won't be for - giv - en 'til I can break
E5 B5 C5 F♯5 G5 F♯5 E5 E5 B5 C5 F♯5 G5 F♯5 E5
free.
Gtr. 7
8va
f w/dist.
full
Gtrs. 5+6
P.M.
P.M.
cont. in slashes

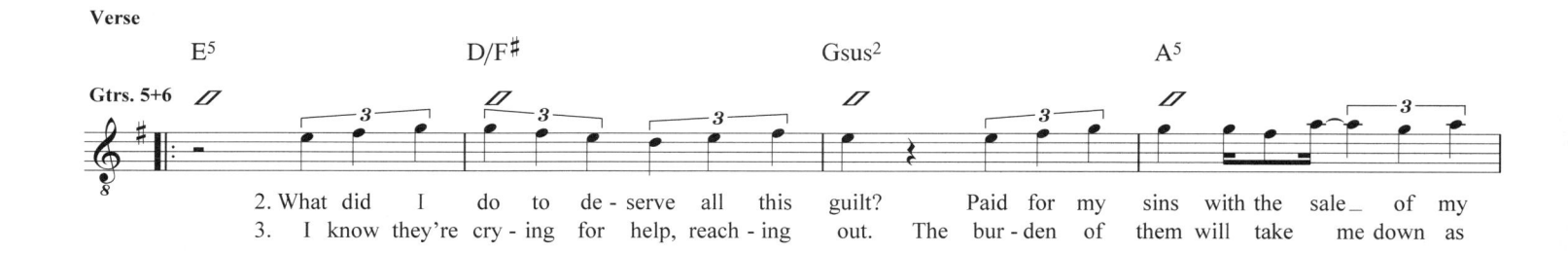

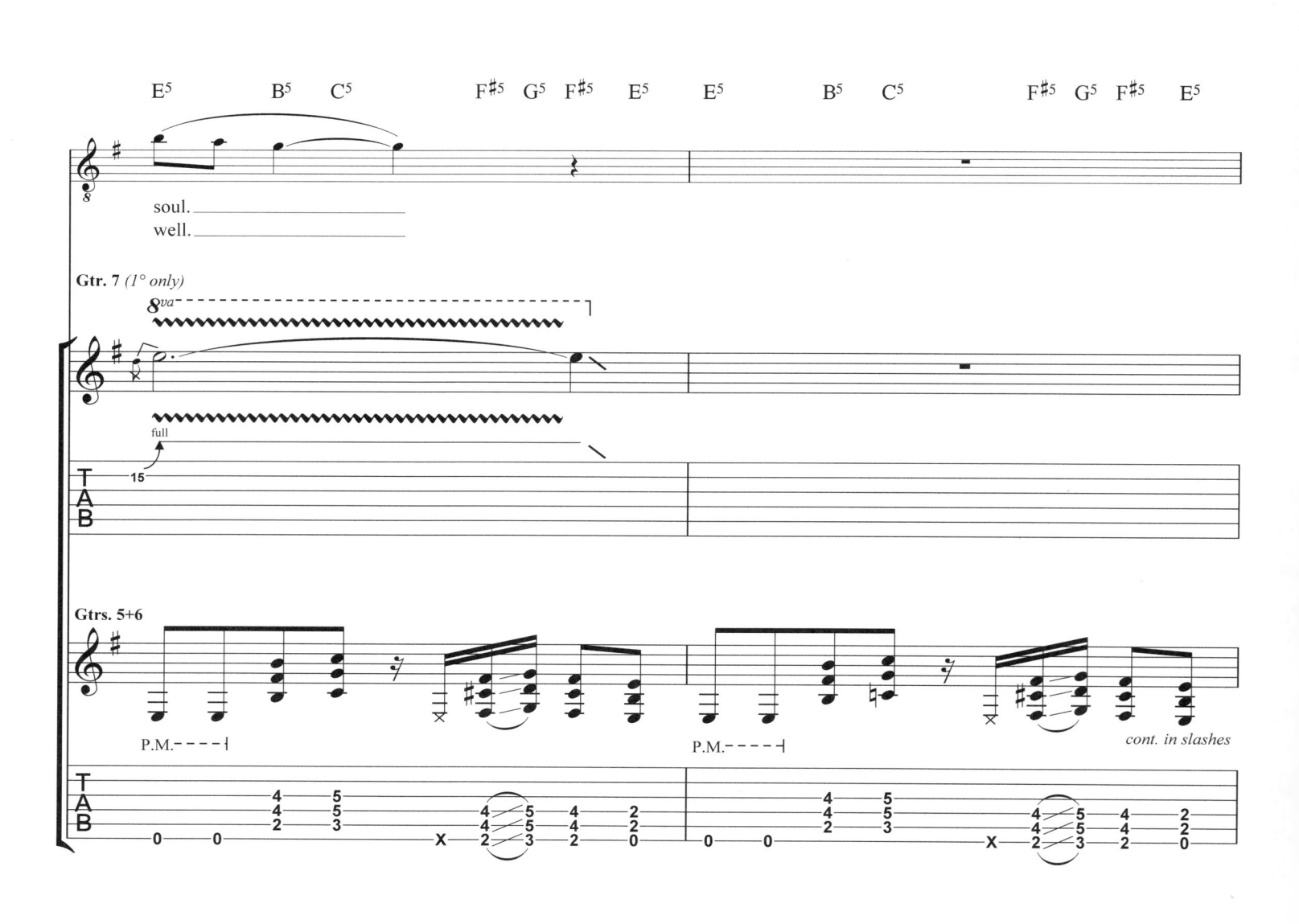

2. What did I do to deserve all this guilt? Paid for my sins with the sale of my soul.
3. I know they're crying for help, reaching out. The burden of them will take me down as well.

De- mons are trapped all in - side of my head, my hopes of God, reach for hea - ven from
The sin of a thou - sand souls, not died in vain. re - in - carn - ates to let me, live a -

hell.
- gain.

Chorus

1. My sins are many, My guilt is too hea - vy.
2. Some one to save me, some - thing to save me from my - self.
3. Some one to save me, some - thing to save me from my hell.

63

The pressure of knowing, of how then what I know.
To bring salvation, to exorcise this hell.
a destination away from this nightmare.
P.M.
Fig. 2
1. I'm able to see things, things I don't want to see.
2. 3. Someone to save me, something to save me from myself.
Gtr. 7
Gtrs. 5+6 play Fig. 2
full
To Coda
1.
The lives of a thousand souls weigh heavy down on me.
To bring salvation, to exorcise this hell.
Gtrs. 5+6

2.
Interlude
C5 D5 E5
1° only
C5 B5 E5 D5 E5 C5 B5 E5 G5 F♯5 E5
P.M.
Play 3 times
C5 B5 E5
C5 B5 E5 D5 E5 C5 B5 E5 G5 F♯5 E5
C5 B5 E5
E5 C5 A5 F5
Gtrs. 5+6
Gtr. 7
cont. in slashes
E5 C5 A5 F5
Play 3 times
Gtr. 8
Gtr. 9

Gtr. 8
E5 C5 A5 F5
Gtr. 7
Gtr. 8
Gtr. 9
E5 C5 A5 F5
Gtrs. 5+6
E5 F5* E5* E5 A5* G♯5 E5 C5* B5* E5 A5* G♯5
P.M.
Gtrs. 7+8+9 tacet
Gtr. Solo
E5 G/B C5
Gtrs. 5+6
P.M.
Gtr. 9
f w/dist.
3

D/F♯
Gsus2
rhythm cont. sim.
E5
G/B
C5
D/F♯
D5
8va
E5
G/B
C5
D/F♯
Gsus2
full
1/2

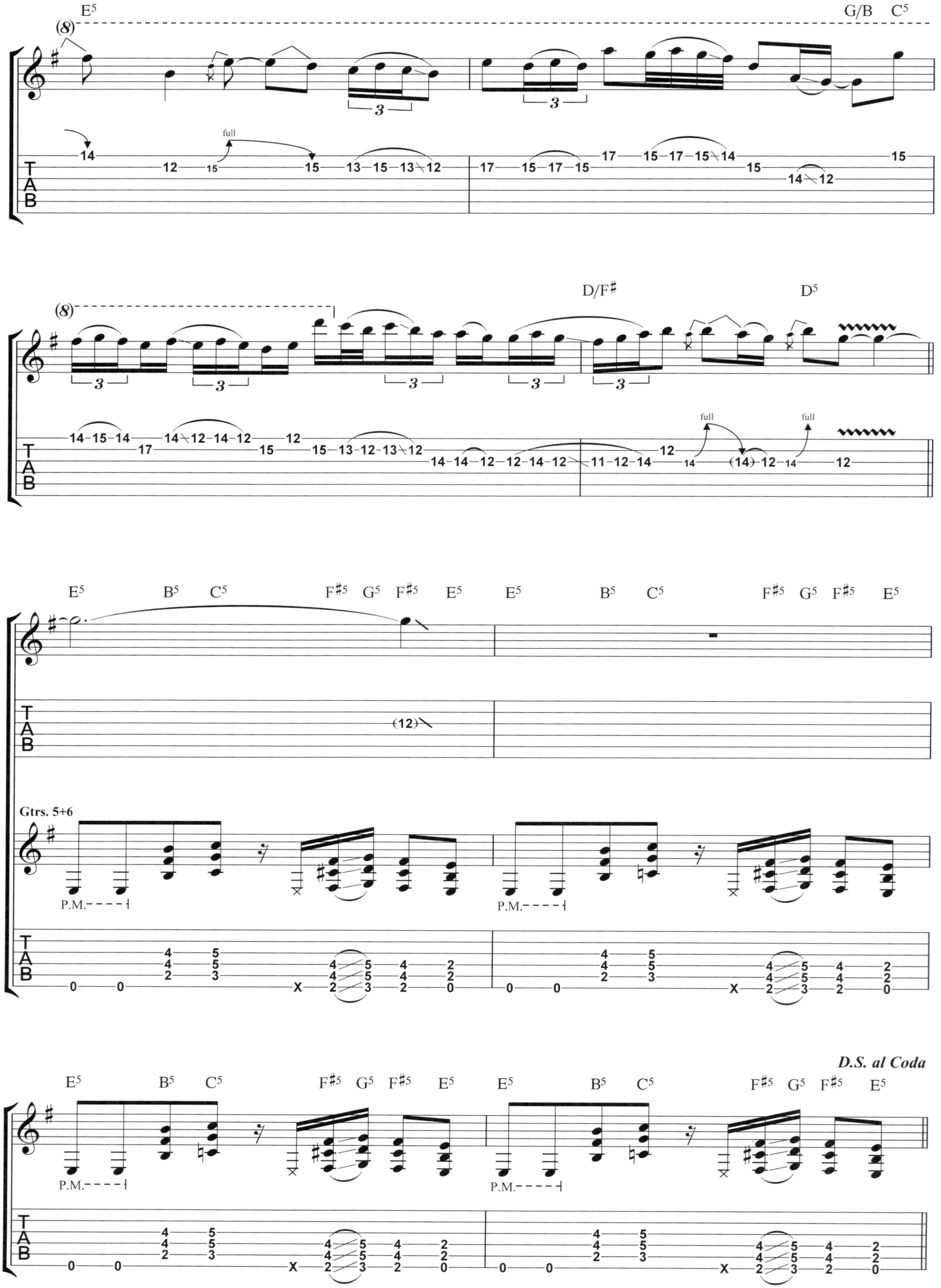
E5
G/B C5
(8)
full
D/F♯
D5
E5 B5 C5 F♯5 G5 F♯5 E5
Gtrs. 5+6
P.M.
D.S. al Coda

Coda
E5 B5 C5 F♯5 G5 F♯5 E5 E5 B5 C5 F♯5 G5 F♯5 E5 E5 B5 C5 F♯5 G5 F♯5 E5
Gtrs. 5+6
P.M.
E5 B5 C5 F♯5 G5 F♯5 E5 E5 F5* E5* E5 A5* G♯5 E5 C5* B5* E5 A5* G♯5
E5 F5* E5* E5 A5* G♯5 E5 C5* B5* E5 A5* G♯5
Gtrs. 5+6 tacet
Outro
Gtr. 4
(E5)
rall.
Harm.
mf let ring...
w/clean tone + chorus
Gtr. 3
mf let ring...
w/clean tone

FOR THE GREATER GOOD OF GOD

Words & Music by
Steve Harris

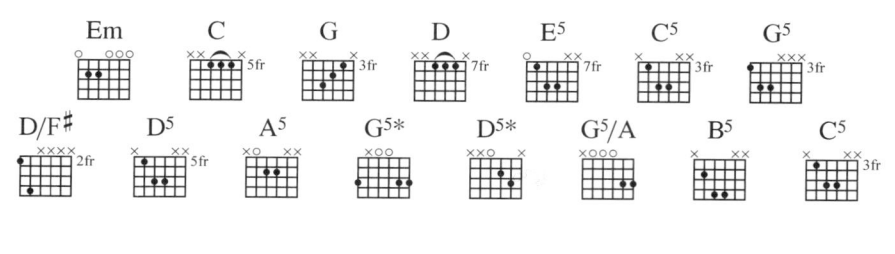

© Copyright 2006 Iron Maiden Publishing (Overseas) Limited.
BMG Music Publishing Limited.
All Rights Reserved. International Copyright Secured.

♩ = 164

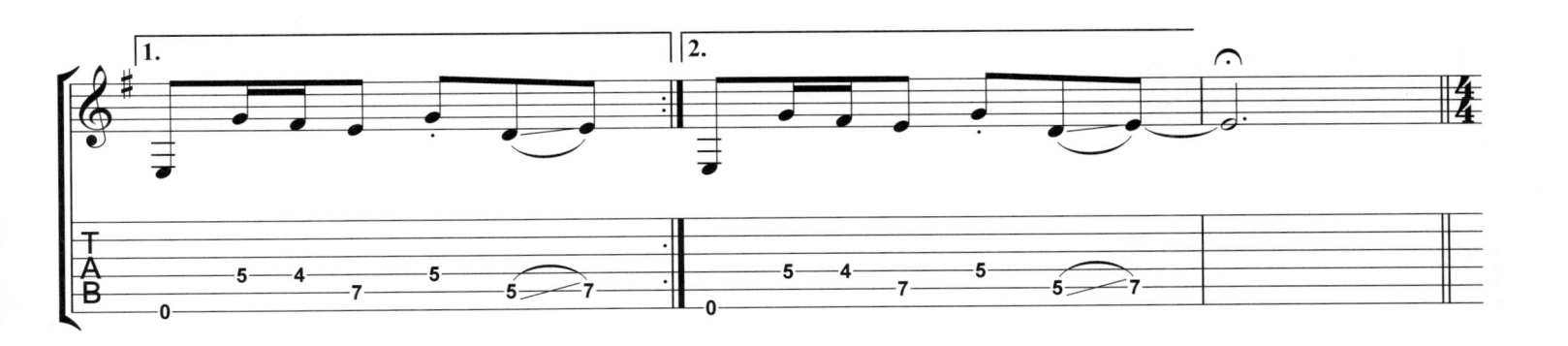

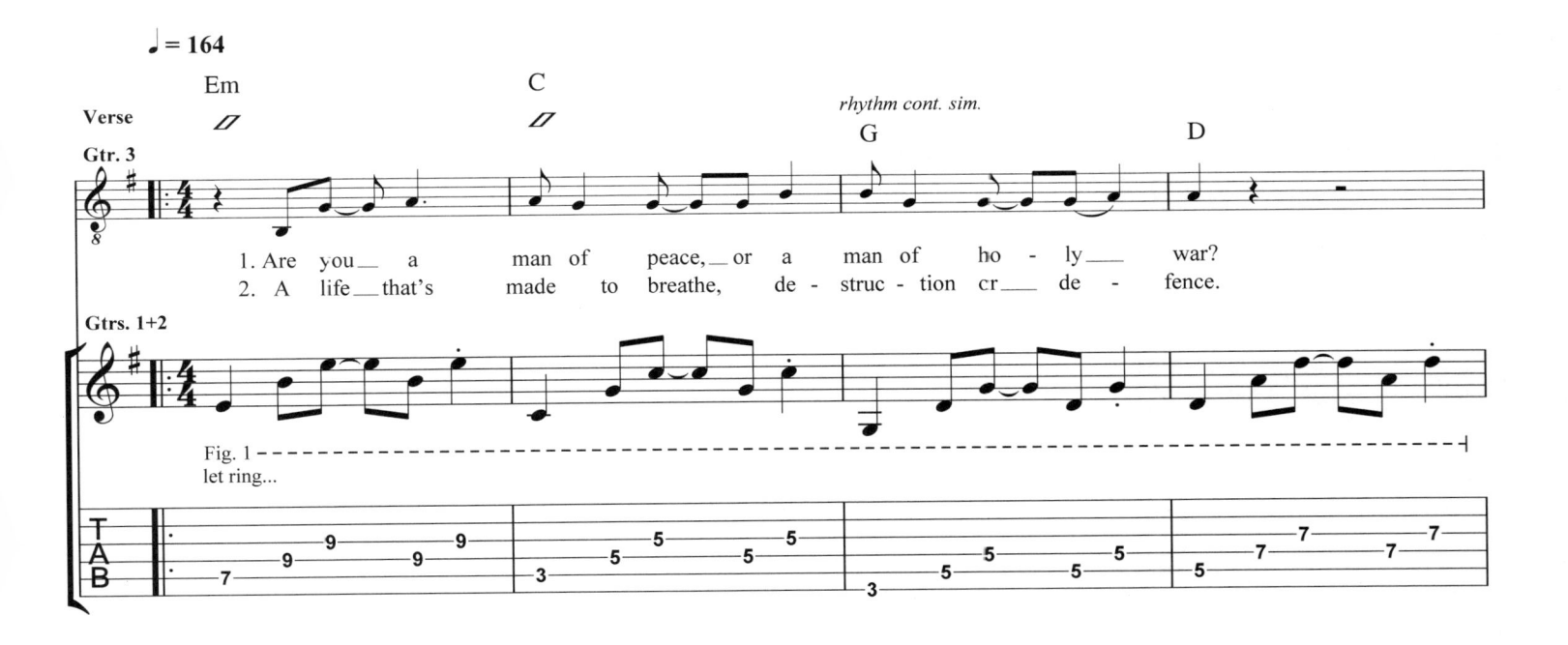

Verse

Em C G D

rhythm cont. sim.

1. Are you a man of peace, or a man of holy war?
2. A life that's made to breathe, destruction cr— de-fence.

Fig. 1
let ring...

Em C G D

Too many sides to you, don't know which any-more.
A mind that's vain cor-rup-tion, bad or good in-tent.

Em C G D

So many full of life, but al-so filled with pain.
A wolf in sheep's cloth-ing, a saint-ly or sin-ner.

Em C G D

Don't know just how many will live to breathe a-gain.
Or some that would be-lieve, a ho-ly war win-ner.

71

3. They fire off many shots and many parting blows.
4. More pain and misery in the hist'ry of mankind.

Their actions beyond a reas'ning, only God would know.
sometimes it seems more like the blind leading the blind.

And as he lies in heaven, or
It brings upon us more of

Lyrics:

it could be__ in__ hell. I feel__ he's
fam - ine, death__ and__ war. You know__ re -

some - where here,__ or look - ing from__ be - low,__ but I don't
-li - gion has__ a lot to ans - wer for.____

Pre-Chorus *Play 1° only*

know.__ I don't know.

♩= 105
Chorus
*E5
C5
G5
D5
Please tell me now what life is.
Please tell me now what love is.
Gtr. 3
cont. sim.
P.M.
Fig. 4
T A B
Fig. 3
*chords implied by bass
Gtrs. 1+2 play Fig. 3
Gtr. 4 plays Fig. 4
E5
A5
C5
D5
Well, tell me now what war is.
A - gain tell me what life is.
♩= 164
Verse
E5
C5
G5
D5
5. And as they searched to find the bo - dies in the sand.
6. And all be - cause of it, you'd think that we'd have learned.
Gtr. 3 (2° only)
Gtrs 1+2 play Fig. 2
Gtr. 1 (2° only)
P.M.

They find it's ashes that are scattered across the land.
But still the body count, the city fires burned.

And as their spirits seemed to whistle on the wind,
Somewhere there's someone dying in a foreign land,

a shot is fired somewhere, another war begins.
meanwhile the world is crying, stupidity of

man, tell me why, _____ tell me why? _____

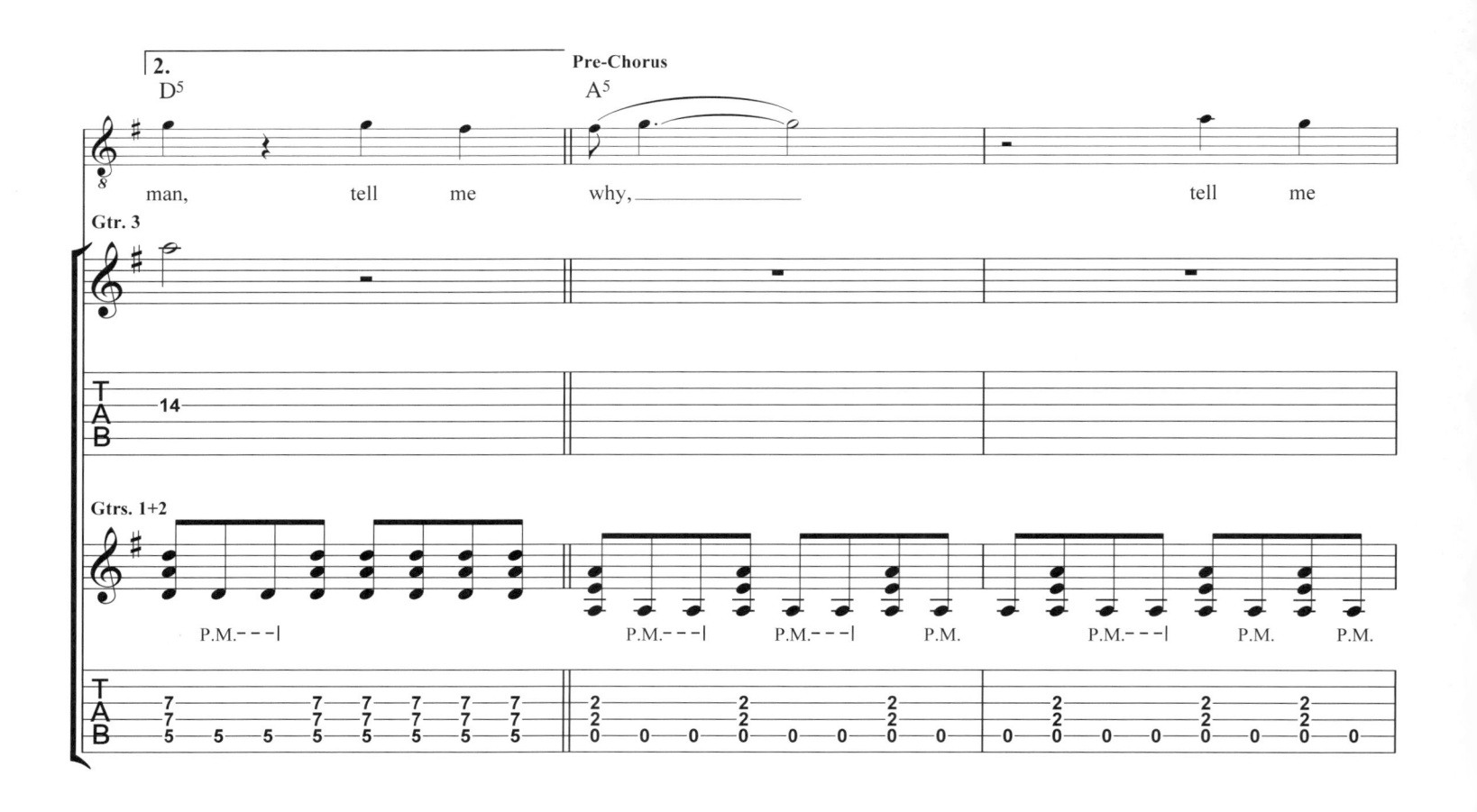

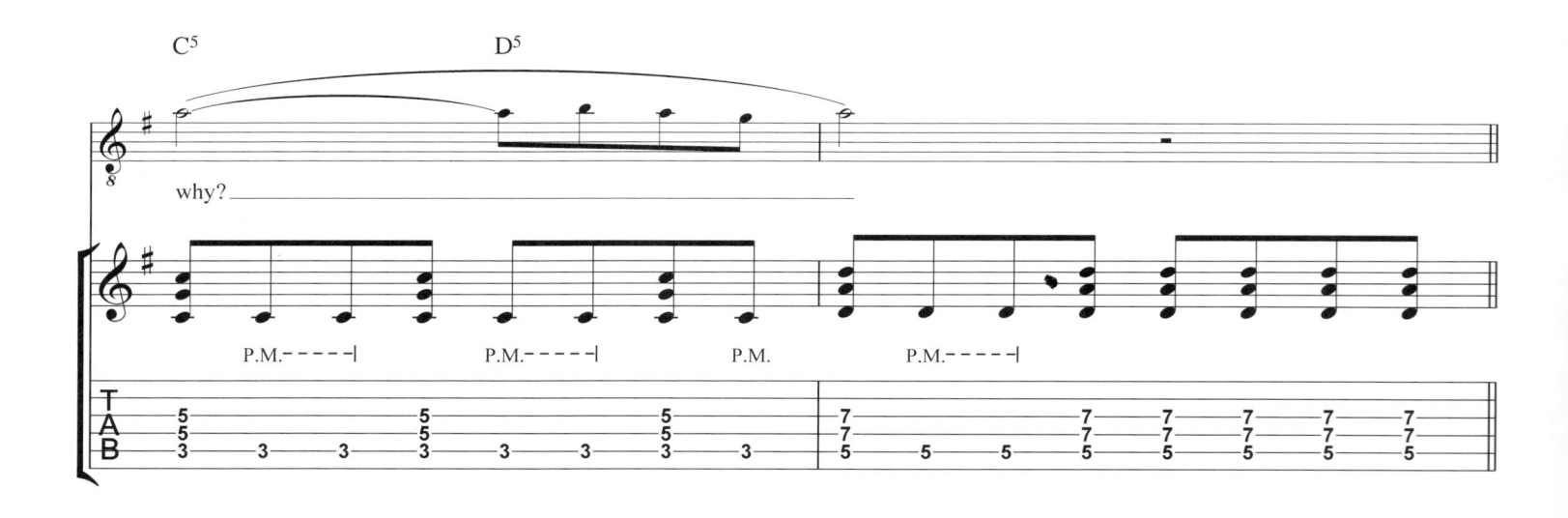

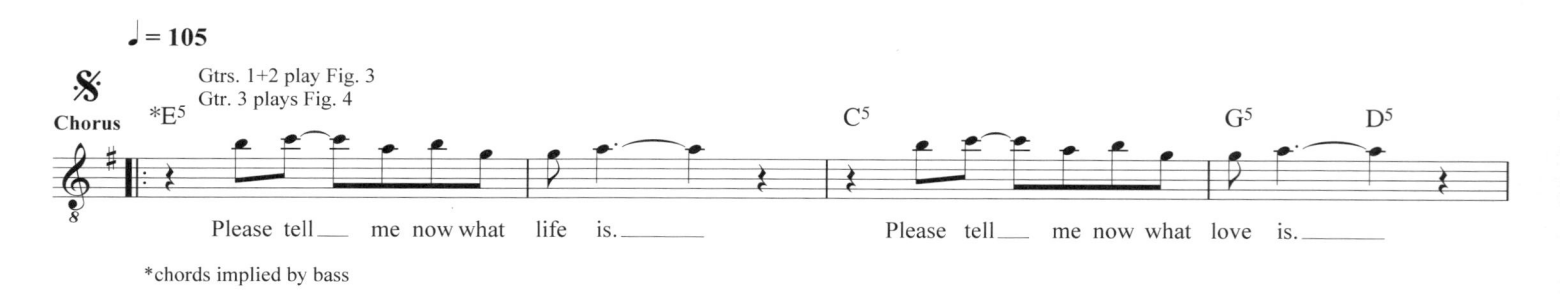

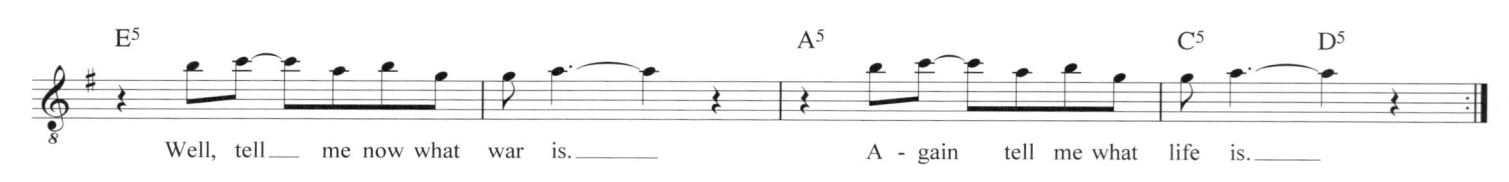

Please tell__ me now what life is.___ Please tell__ me now what love is.___

Well, tell__ me now what war is.___ A - gain tell me what life is.___

Bridge

For the greater good of God.

For the greater good of God. For the greater good of

God. For the greater good of God.

Interlude

*E5
C5
G5
D5
*chords implied by bass
E5
A5
C5
D5
G5*
D5*
Gtr. 3
(E)
Gtr. 2
Gtr. 1
Fig. 7
let ring...
Gtr. 2 cont. in slashes
A5
G5*
G5/A
D5
Fig. 8

Gtr. Solo
(E)
Gtr. 4
8va
rake
ff
Gtr. 4 w/dist.
Gtr. 1 plays Fig. 7
Gtr. 3 plays Fig. 8
full
G5*
D5*
A5
full
G5*
G5/A
D5
full
full
Interlude
(E)
1° only
Gtr. 3 tacet
Gtr. 4 tacet
Gtrs. 1+2
P.M.
Fig. 9

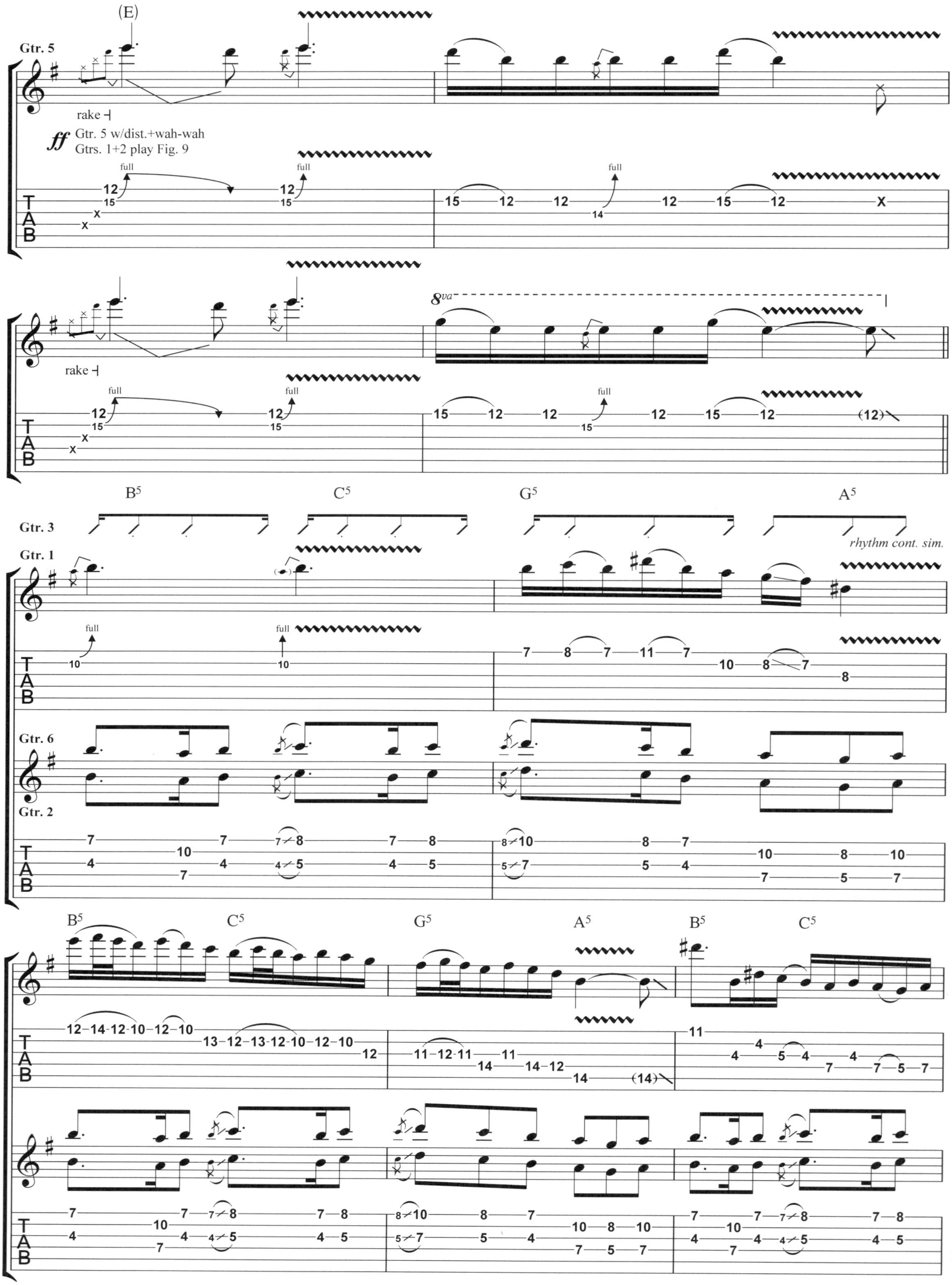
(E)
Gtr. 5
rake
ff
Gtr. 5 w/dist.+wah-wah
Gtrs. 1+2 play Fig. 9
full
8va
B5
C5
G5
A5
Gtr. 3
Gtr. 1
rhythm cont. sim.
Gtr. 6
Gtr. 2
TAB

G5 A5 B5 C5 G5 A5
Gtr. 5
full
(E)
Gtrs. 1+2 play Fig. 9
Gtrs. 3+6 tacet
full
1/2

8va
full
1.
Interlude
B5
C5
G5
A5
B5
C5
Gtrs. 1+3
rhythm cont. sim.
(8)
Gtr. 6
Gtr. 2
2.
G5
A5
B5
C5
G5
A5
Gtr. 3
Gtrs. 1+2
Gtr. 2 cont. in slashes
TAB

1, 2, 3.
4.
D.S. al Coda (with repeats)
E5
C5
Gtr. 4
rhythm cont. sim.
G5
D5
D5
Coda
rall.
C5
D5
God.
Outro
♩= 164
Em
C
G
D
Gtr. 3
rhythm cont. sim.
He gave his life for us, he fell up-on the cross.
Gtrs. 1+2
(Fig. 1)
mf let ring...
w/clean tone + chorus

Gtrs 1+2 play Fig. 1
Em C G D
To die for all of those who nev - er mourn his loss.
Em C G D
It was - n't meant for us to feel the pain a - gain. Tell me
A C rit.
why, tell me why?
Gtrs. 1+2
D ♩. = 43 (E) rall.
Gtrs.1+2+3

LORD OF LIGHT

**Words & Music by
Steve Harris, Adrian Smith & Bruce Dickinson**

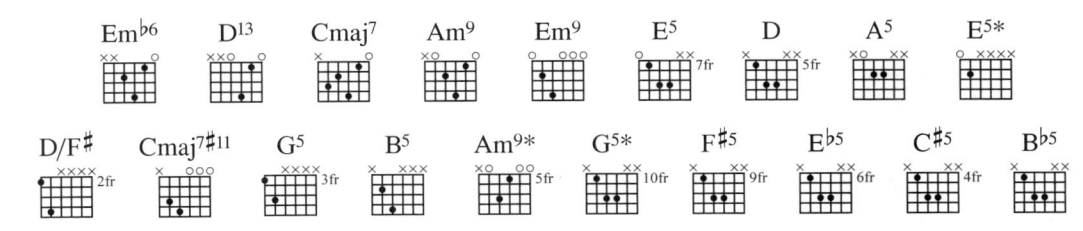

Cmaj7   Am9   **1, 2.** D13

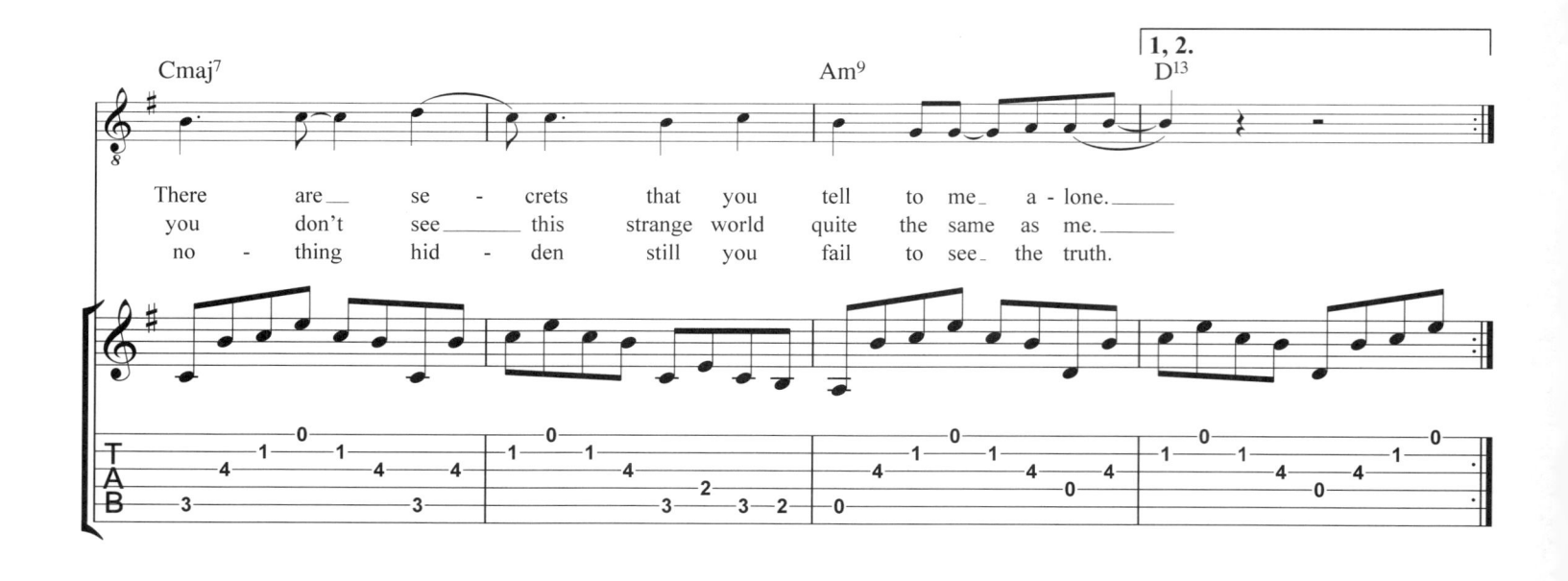

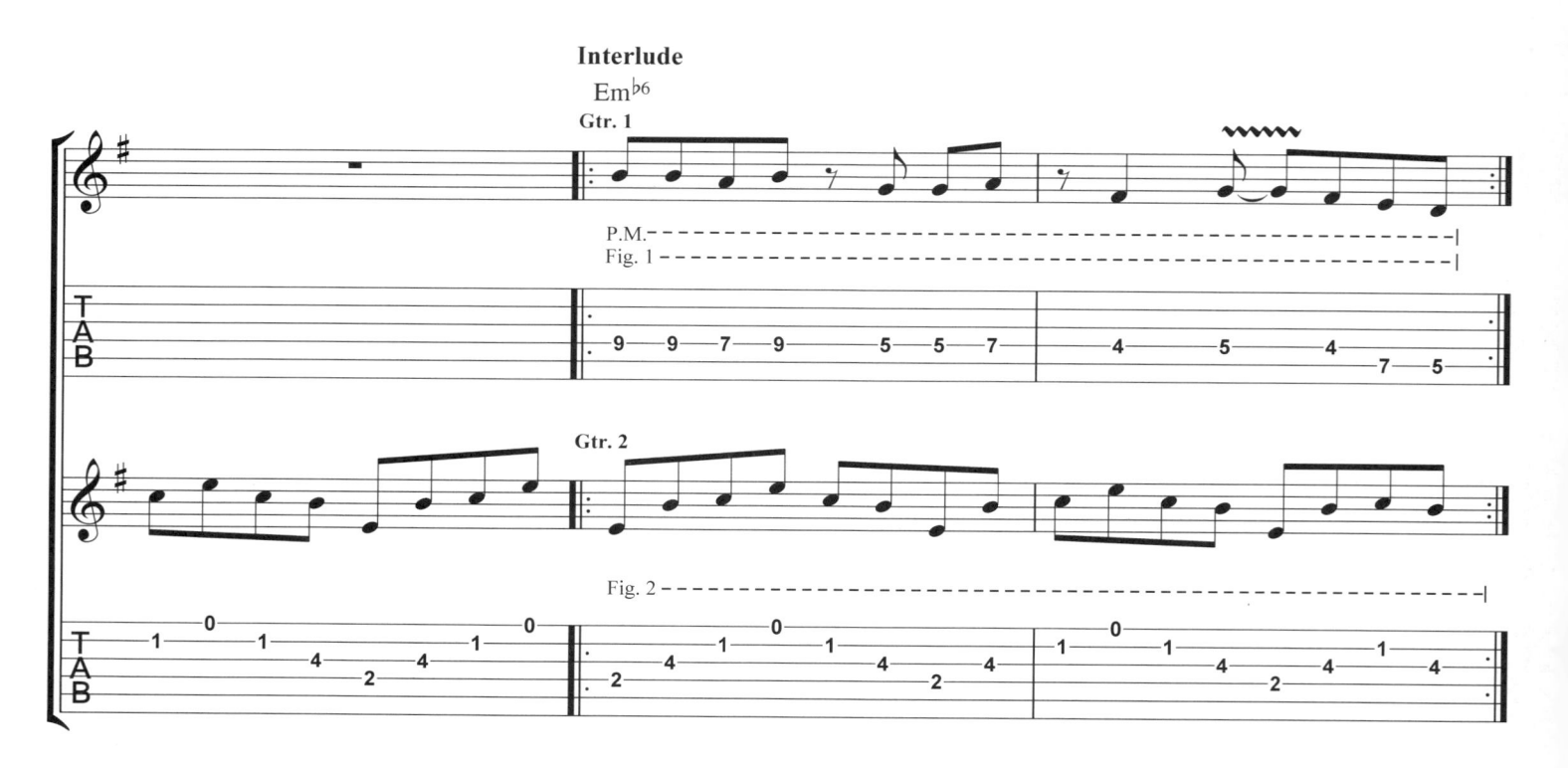

There are se - crets that you tell to me a - lone.
you don't see this strange world quite the same as me.
no - thing hid - den still you fail to see the truth.

3. D13   Em♭6

These are things you can't re - veal.

Interlude

Em♭6

Gtr. 1

P.M.
Fig. 1

Gtr. 2

Fig. 2

These are things you can't re - veal.

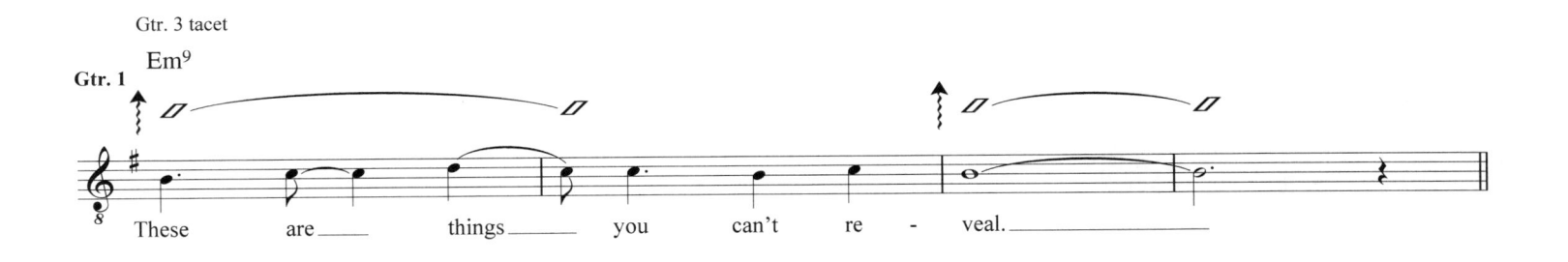

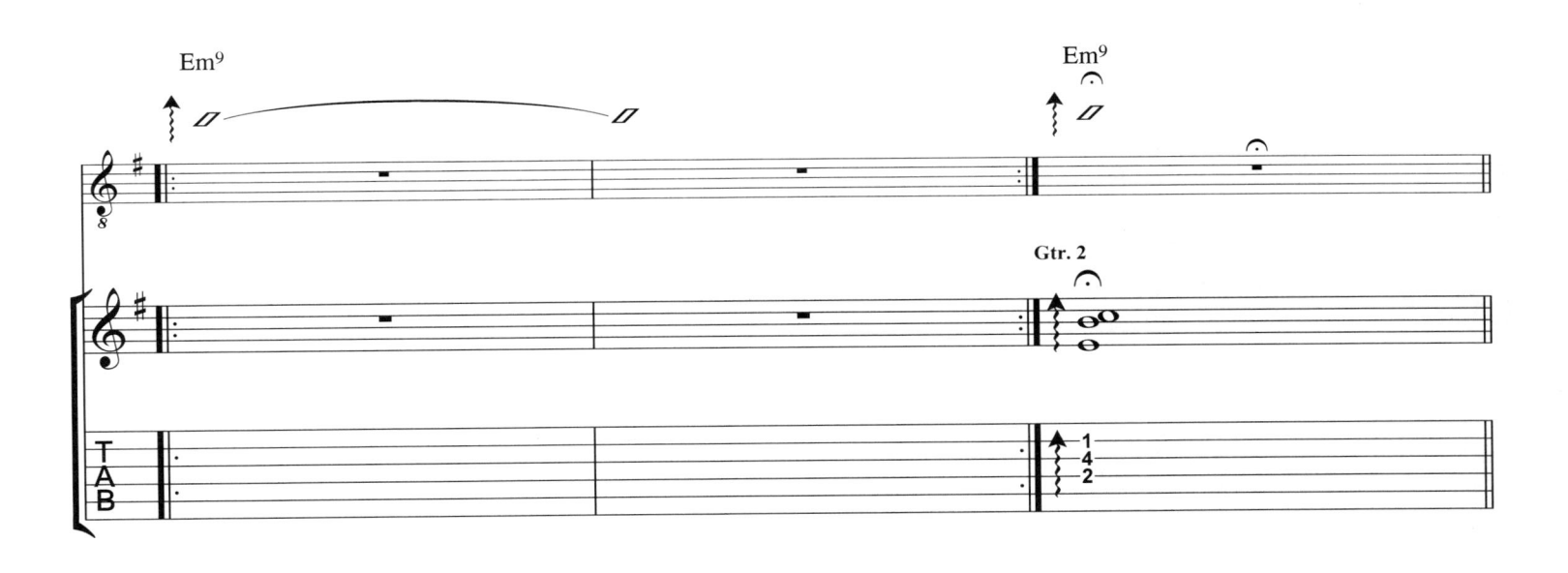

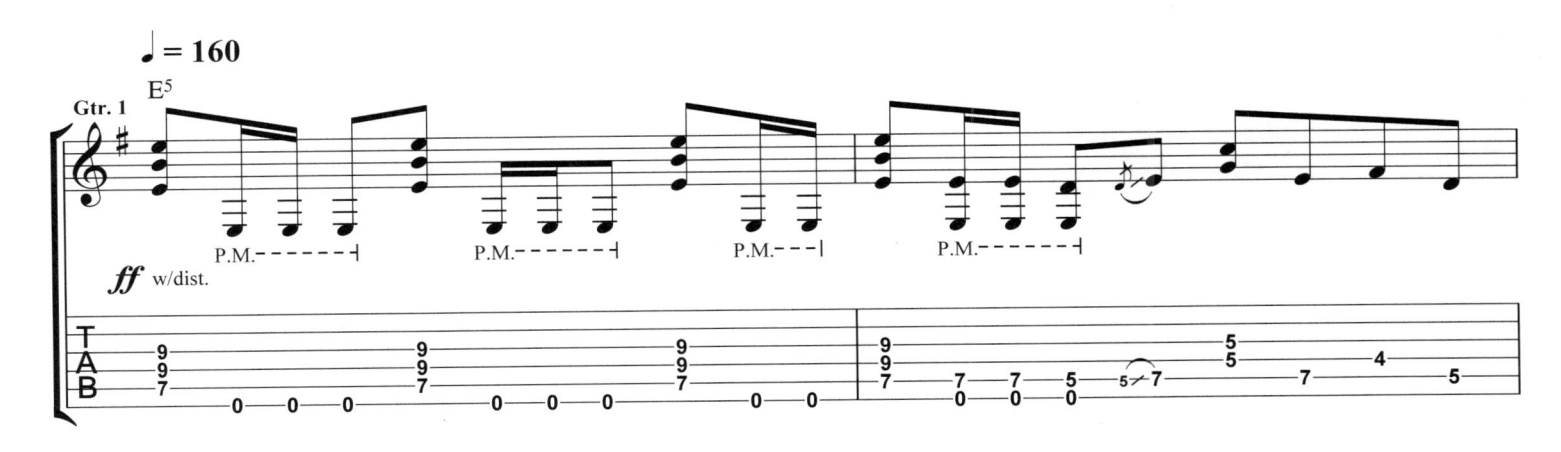

Verse

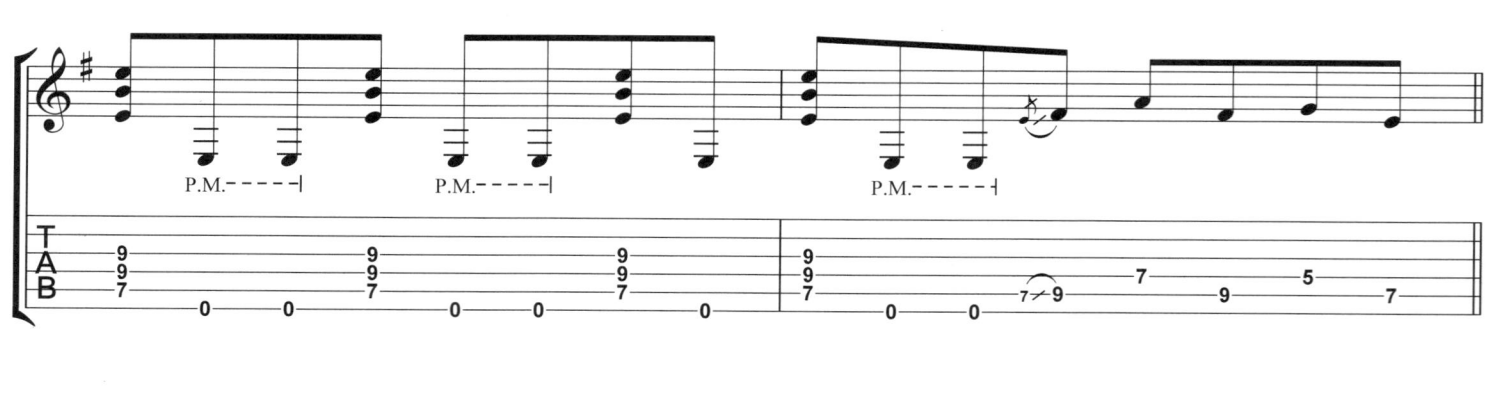

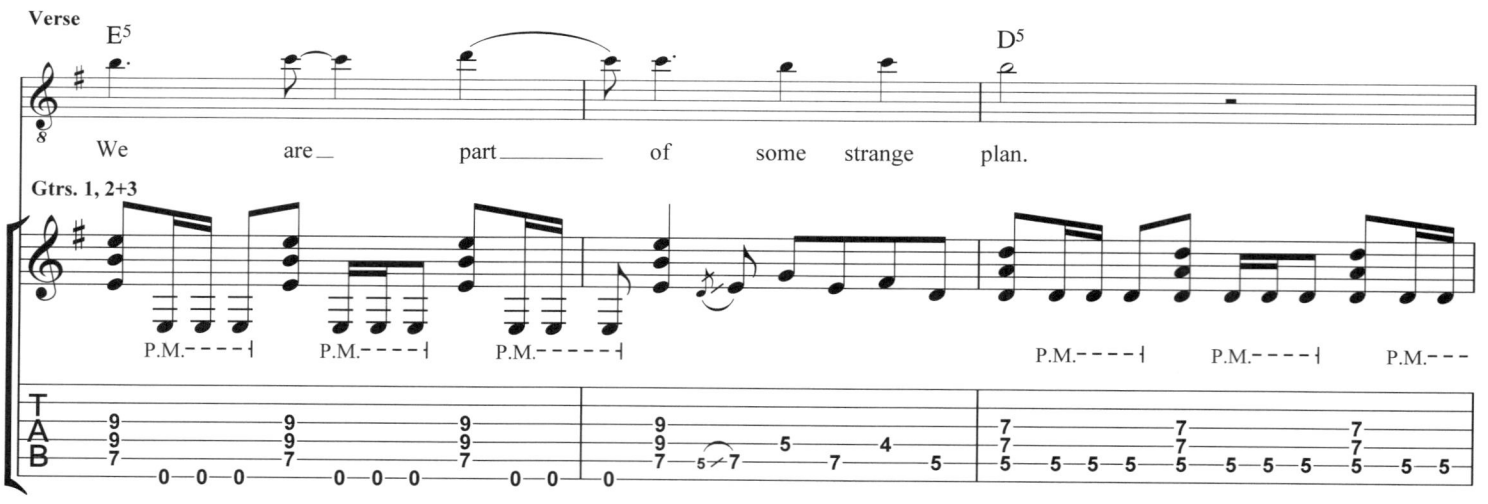

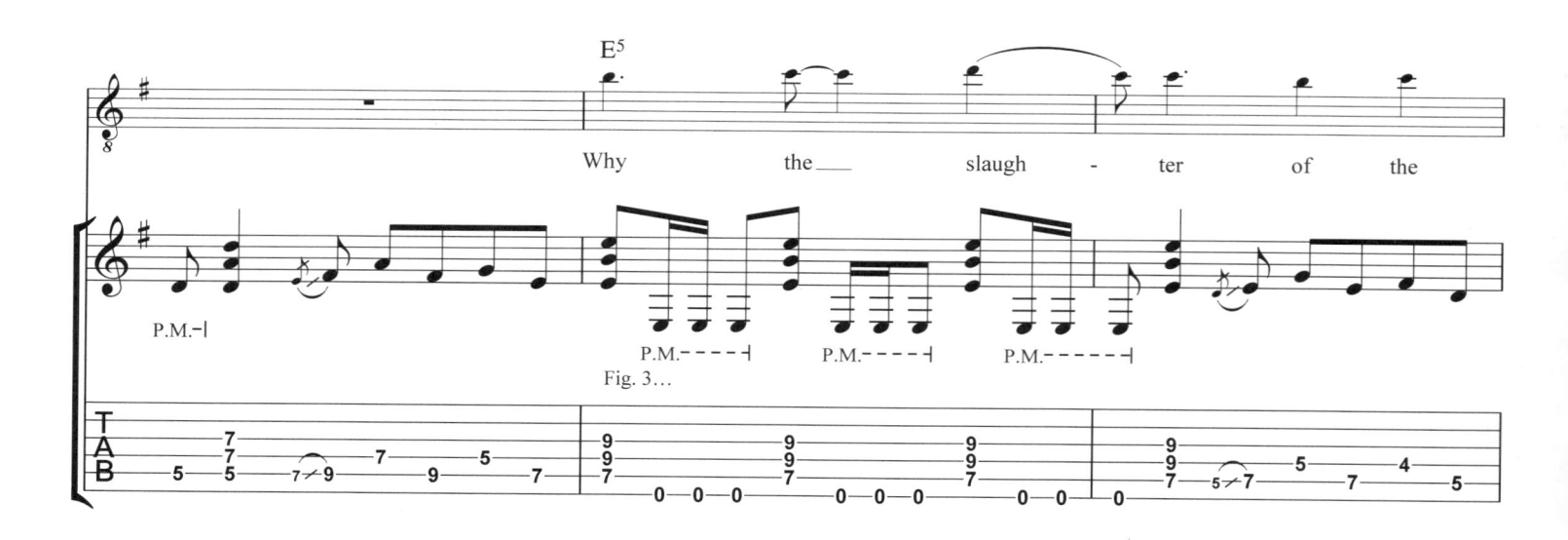

We are part of some strange plan.

Gtrs. 1, 2+3

Why the slaugh-ter of the

Fig. 3...

bro-ther-hood of man? In-fern-al sac-

- ri - fice of hell.

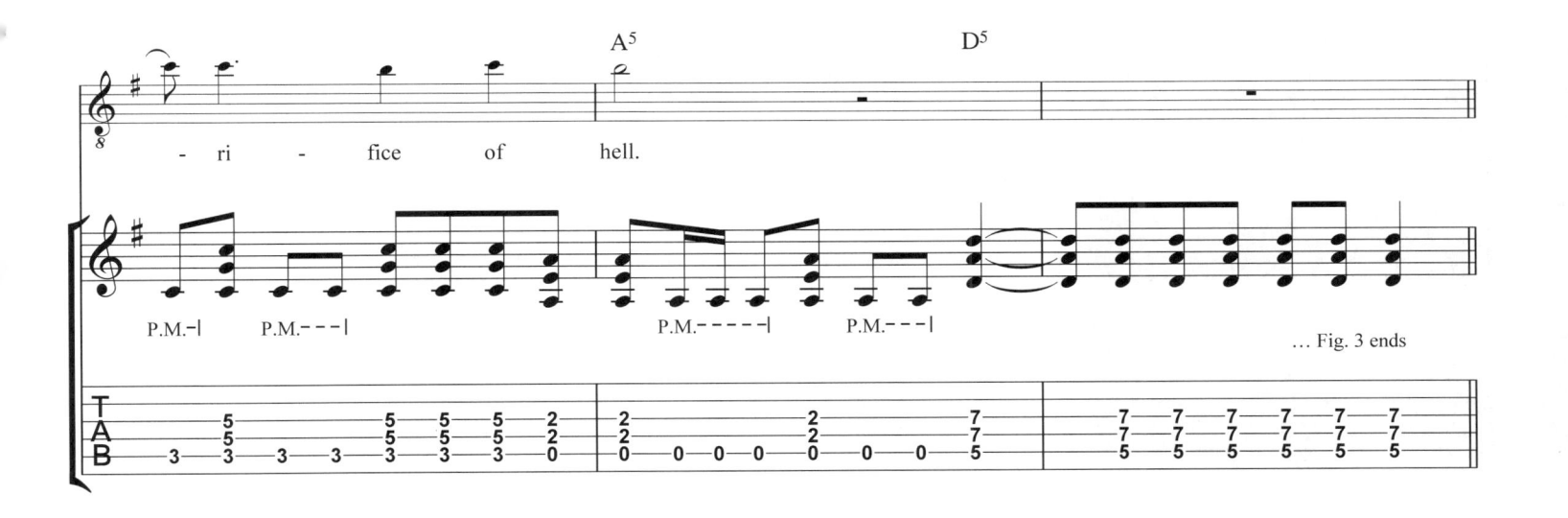

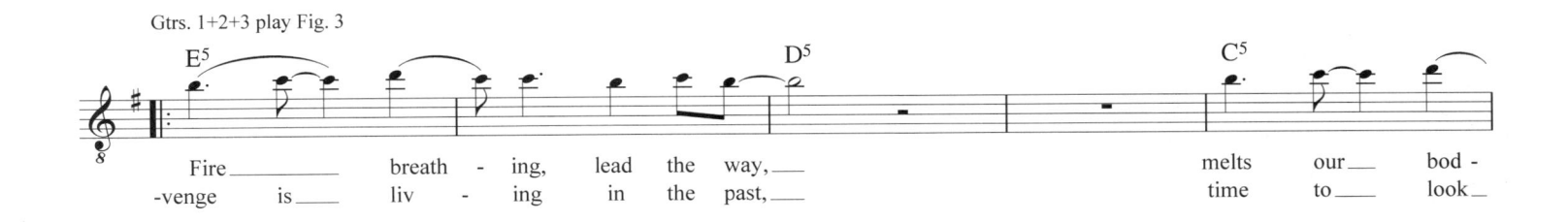

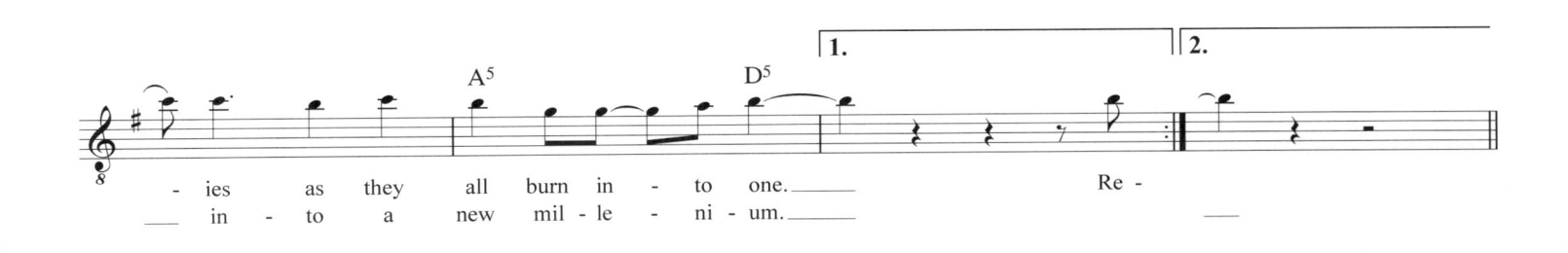

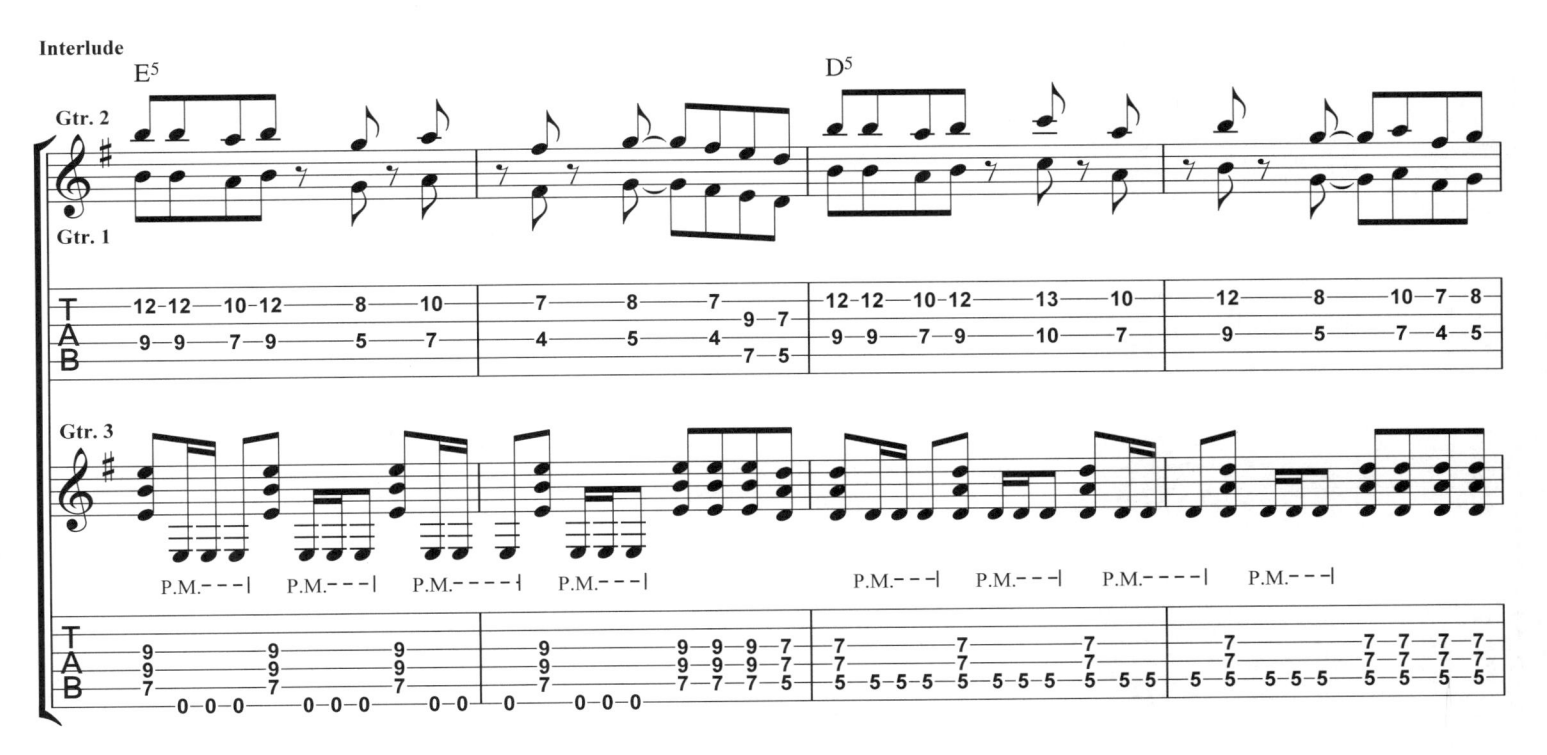

Gtrs. 1+2+3 play Fig. 3

Fire breath - ing, lead the way, melts our bod -
-venge is liv - ing in the past, time to look

- ies as they all burn in - to one. Re -
- in - to a new mil - le - ni - um.

Interlude

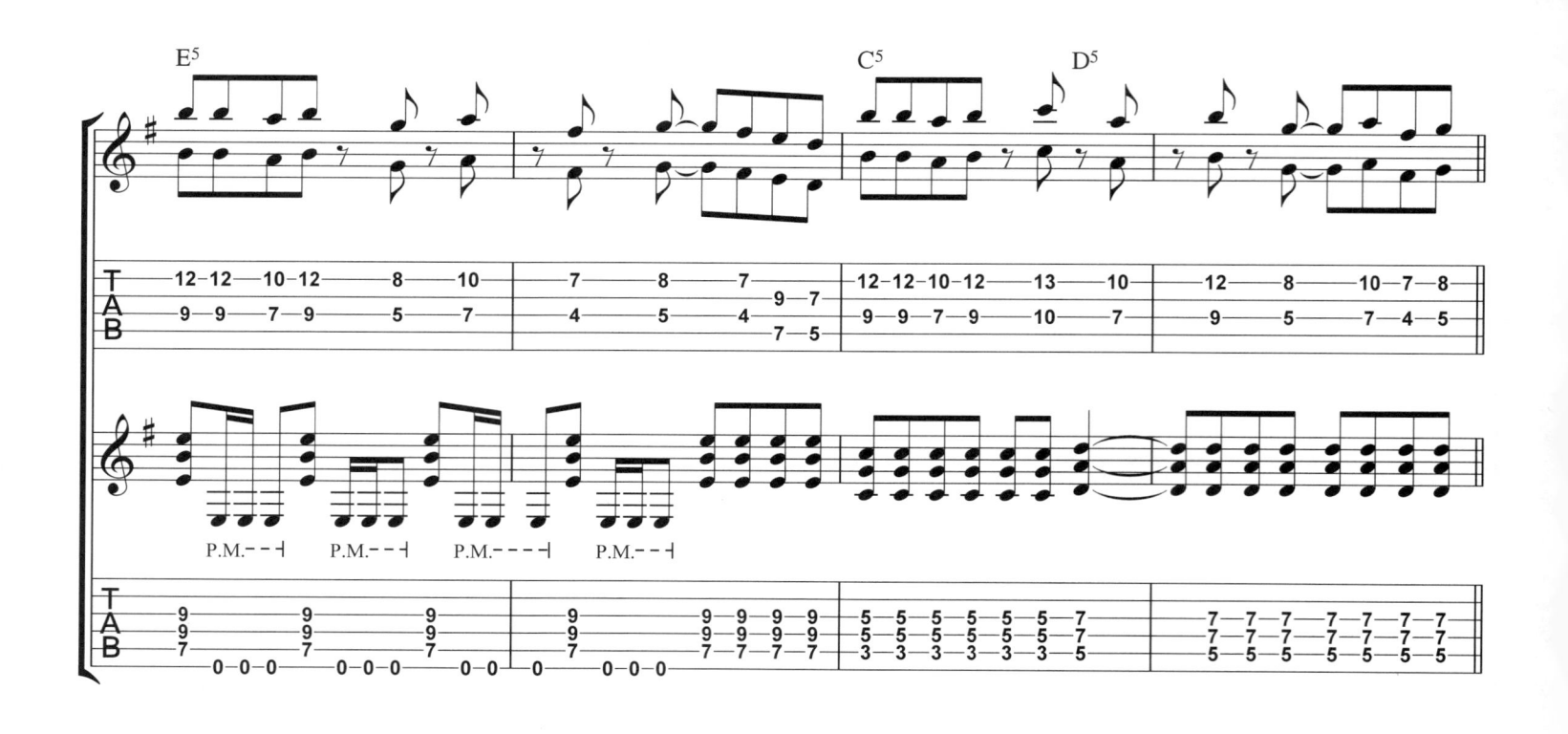

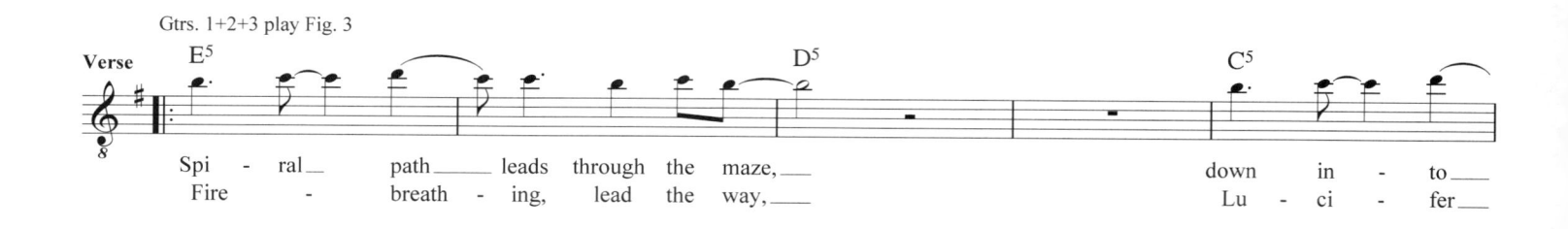

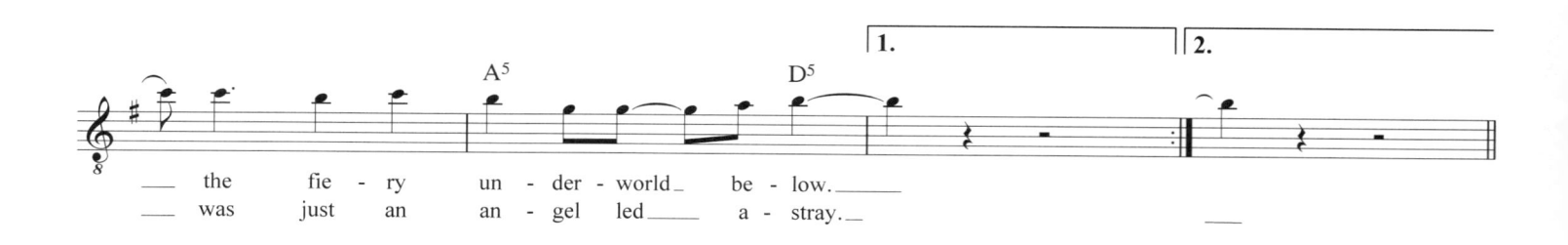

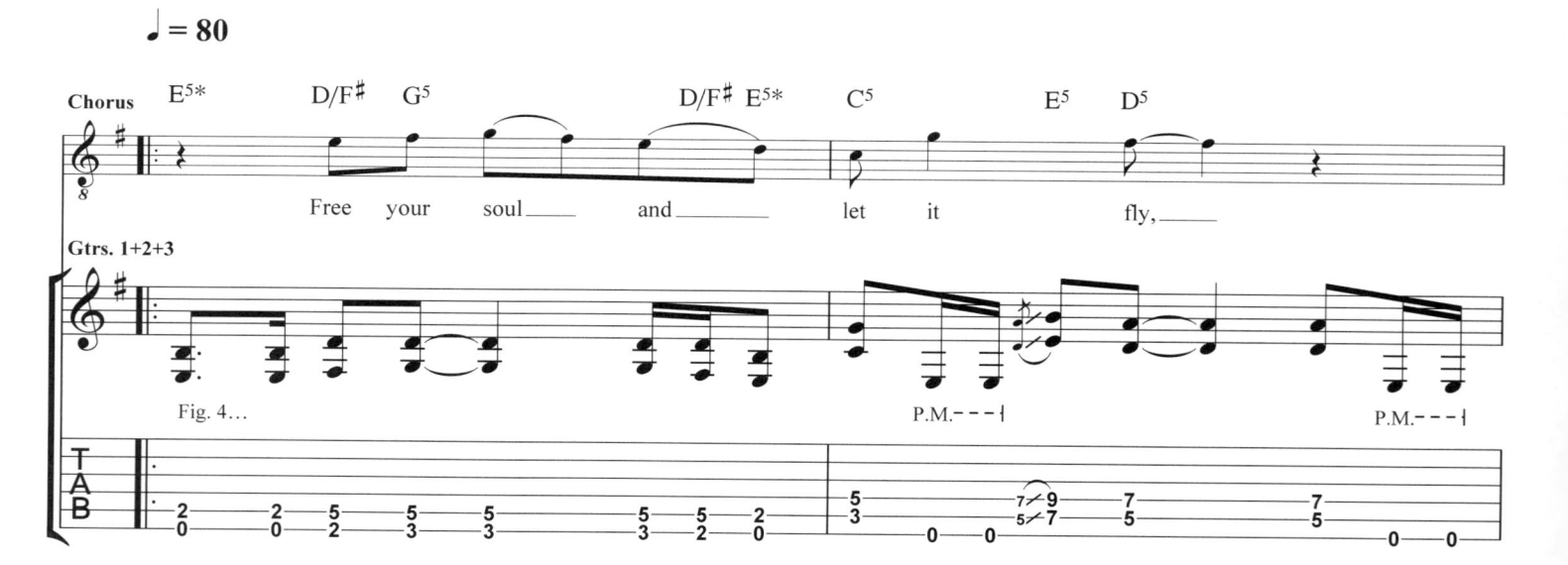

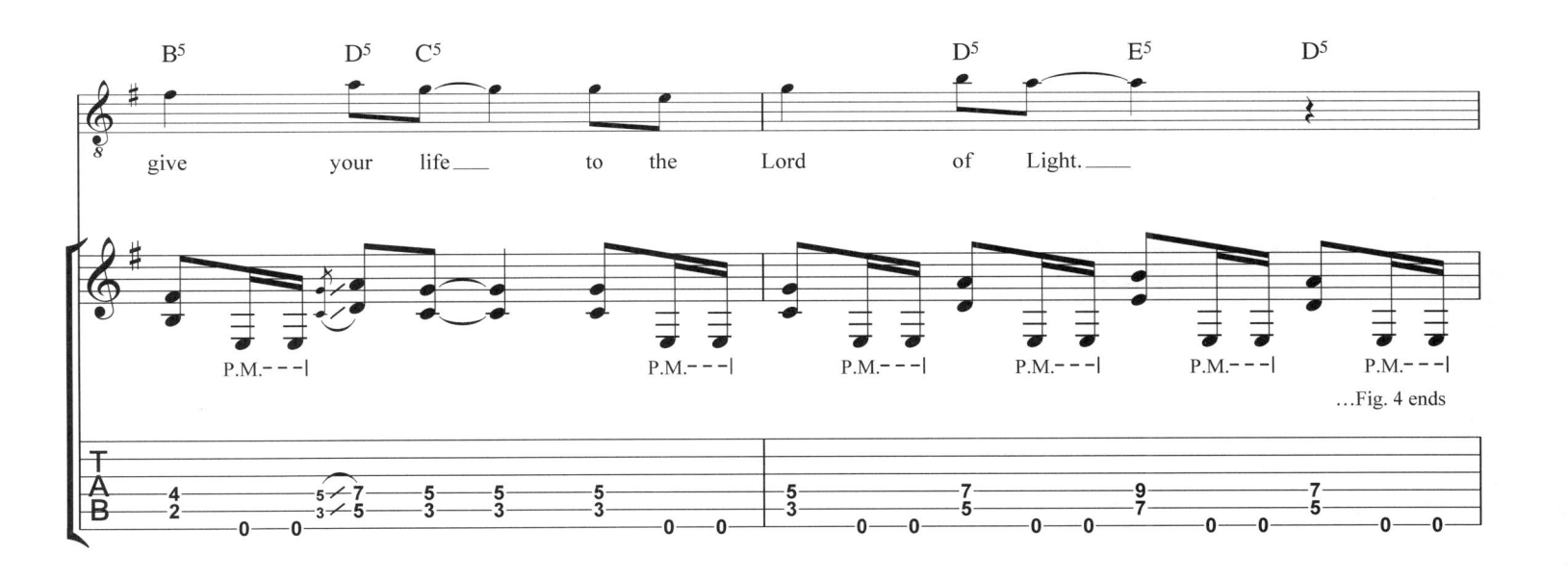

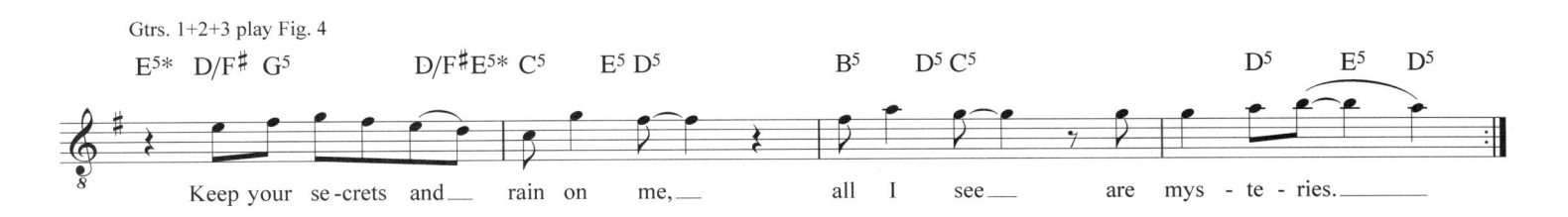

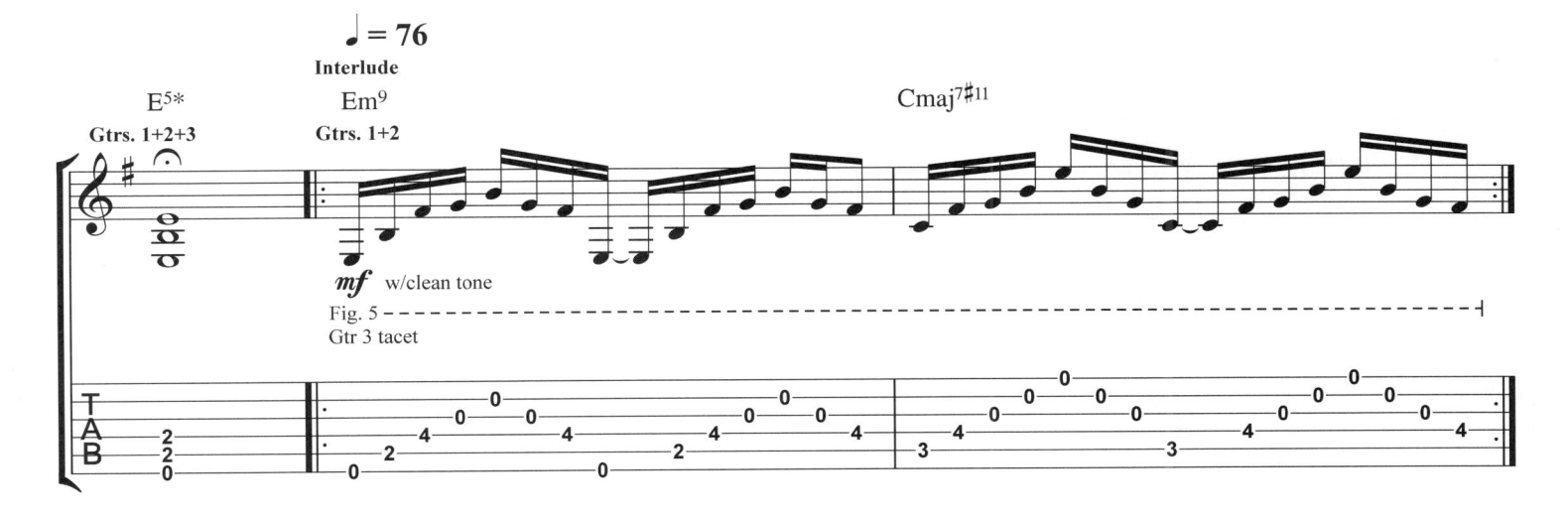

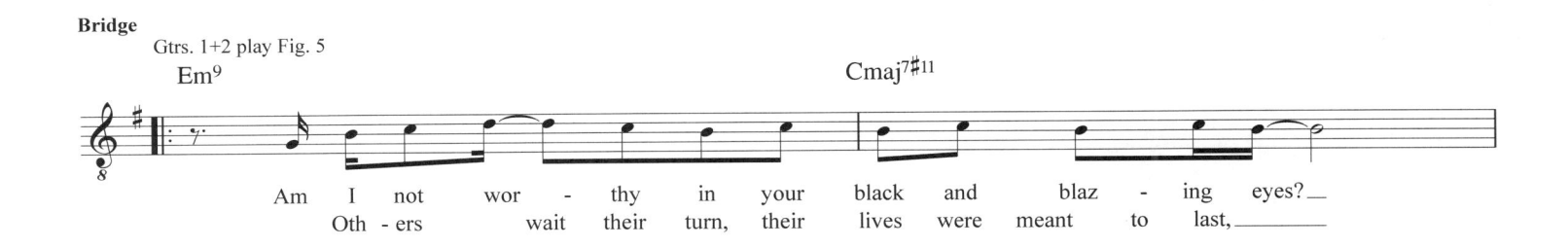

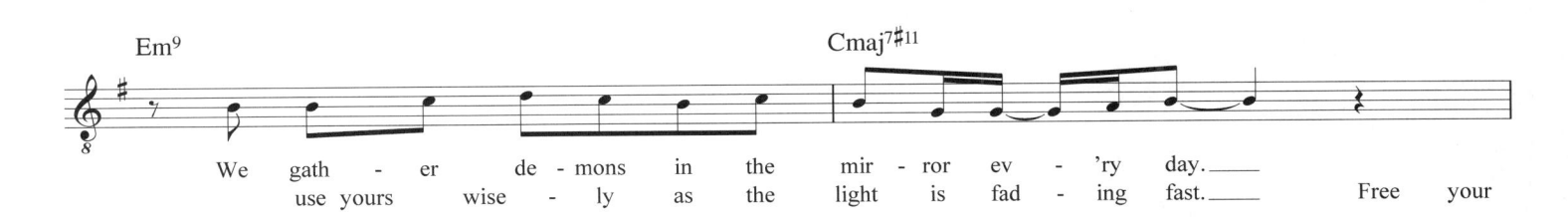

give your life___ to the Lord of Light.___

Keep your se-crets and___ rain on me,___ all I see___ are mys-te-ries.

♩ = 76
Interlude

mf w/clean tone
Fig. 5
Gtr 3 tacet

Bridge
Gtrs. 1+2 play Fig. 5

Am I not wor-thy in your black and blaz-ing eyes?
Oth-ers wait their turn, their lives were meant to last,___

We gath-er de-mons in the mir-ror ev-'ry day.___
use yours wise-ly as the light is fad-ing fast.___ Free your

Am9* Fmaj7♯11
The bridge of darkness casts a shadow on us all,
soul and let it fly, mine was caught, I couldn't try. Time re-
Gtrs. 1+2
Am9 1. Fmaj7♯11
and all our sins to you we give this day.
turns again to punish all of
2. E5 G5* F♯5 E5 C5 E♭5
us.
We were cast out by our bloody father's hand.
We are the shadows of the one unholy ghost.
P.M.
ff w/dist.
E5 G5* F♯5 E5 C5 E♭5
We are strangers in this lonely promised land.
In our nightmare world, the only one we trust.
P.M.

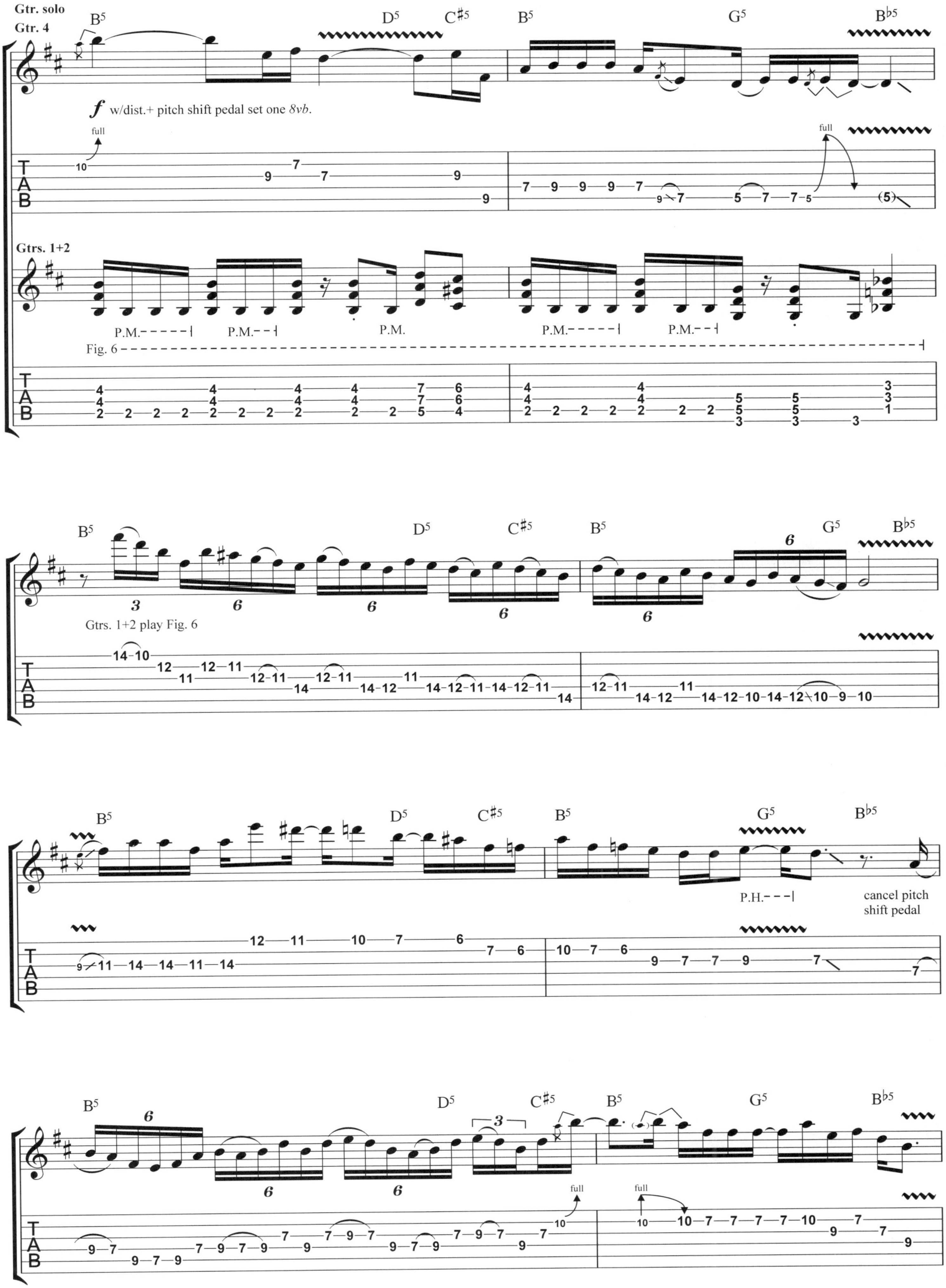
Gtr. solo
Gtr. 4
B5 D5 C#5 B5 G5 Bb5
f w/dist.+ pitch shift pedal set one 8vb.
full
Gtrs. 1+2
P.M.
Fig. 6
Gtrs. 1+2 play Fig. 6
P.H.
cancel pitch shift pedal

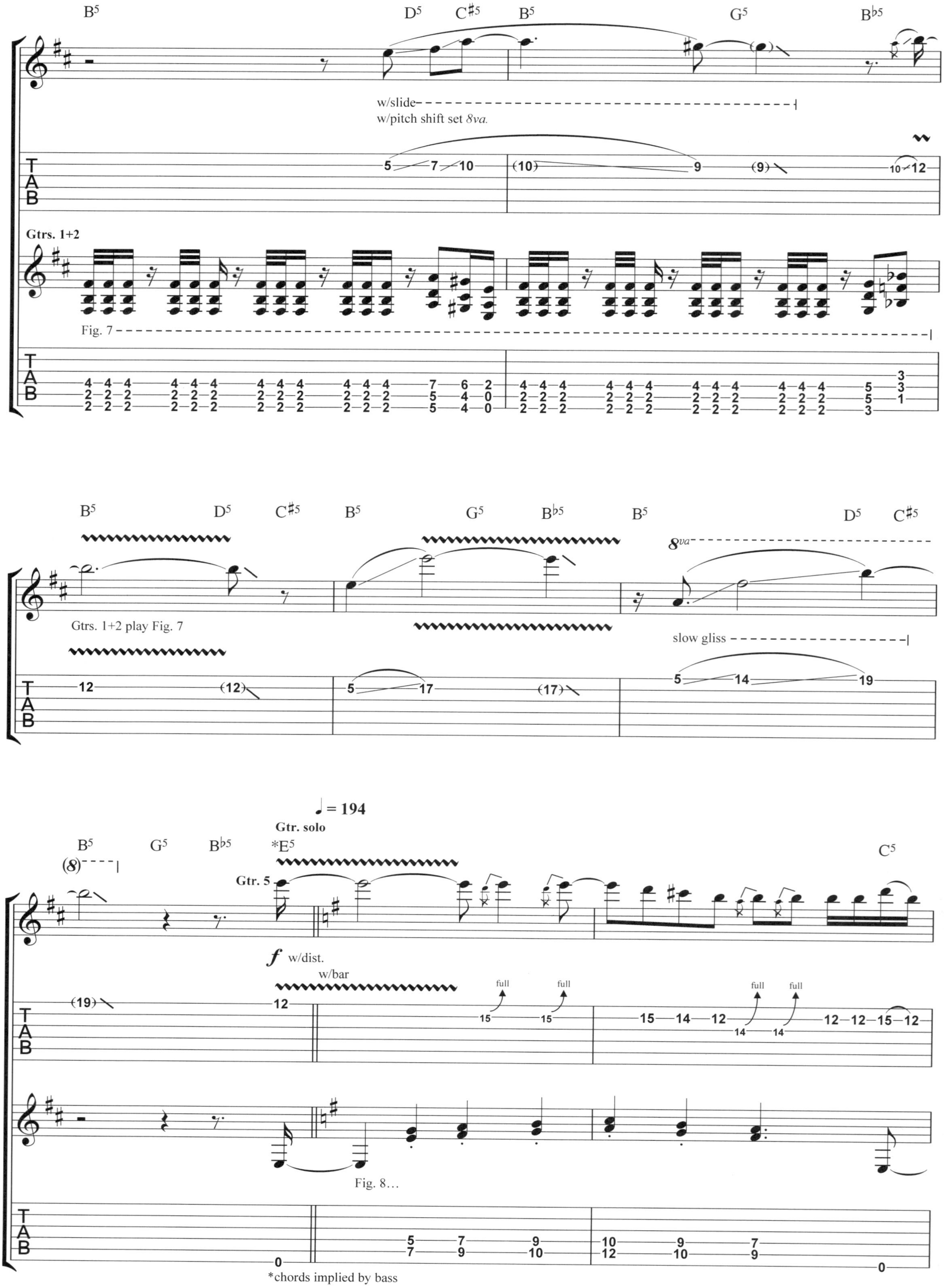
B5 D5 C♯5 B5 G5 B♭5
w/slide
w/pitch shift set 8va.
Gtrs. 1+2
Fig. 7
B5 D5 C♯5 B5 G5 B♭5 B5 D5 C♯5
8va
Gtrs. 1+2 play Fig. 7
slow gliss
♩= 194
Gtr. solo
B5 G5 B♭5 *E5 C5
(8)
Gtr. 5
f w/dist.
w/bar
full
Fig. 8…
*chords implied by bass

95

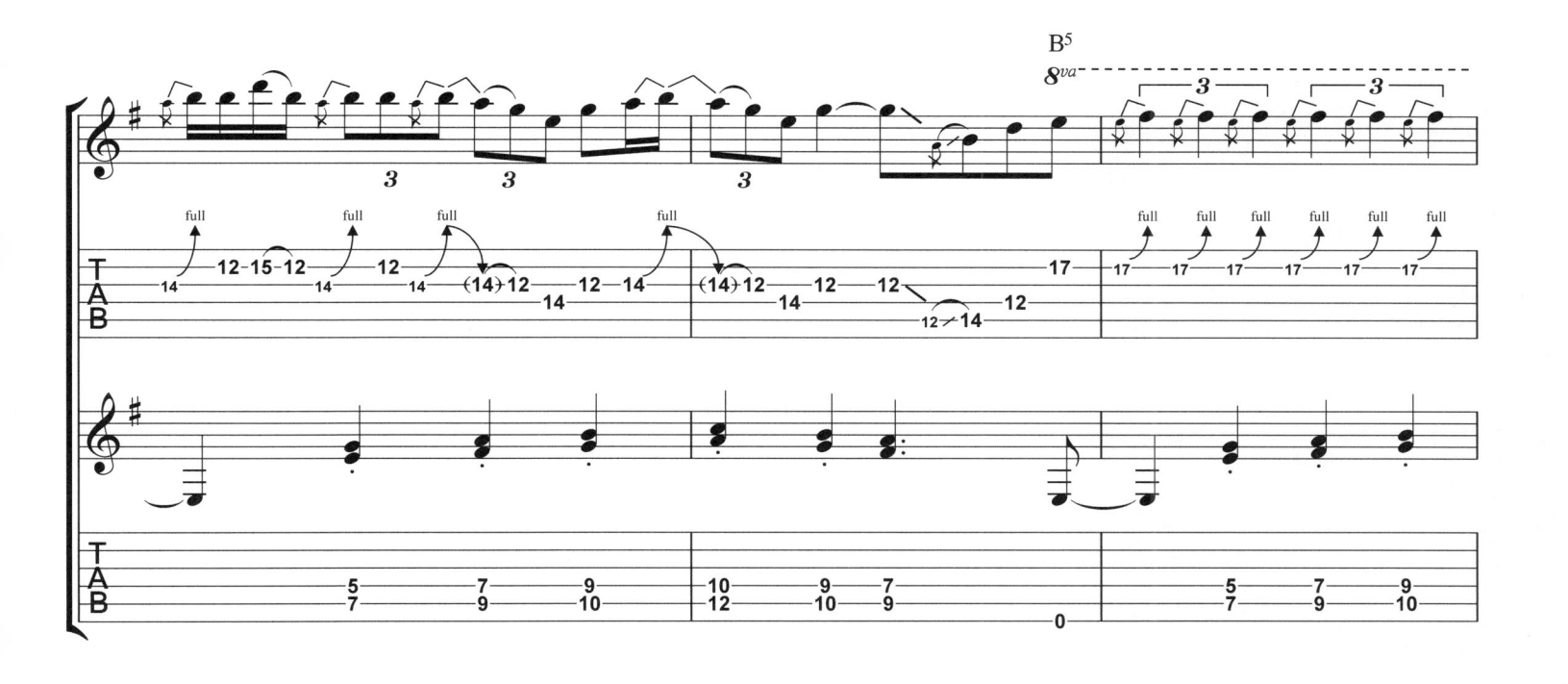

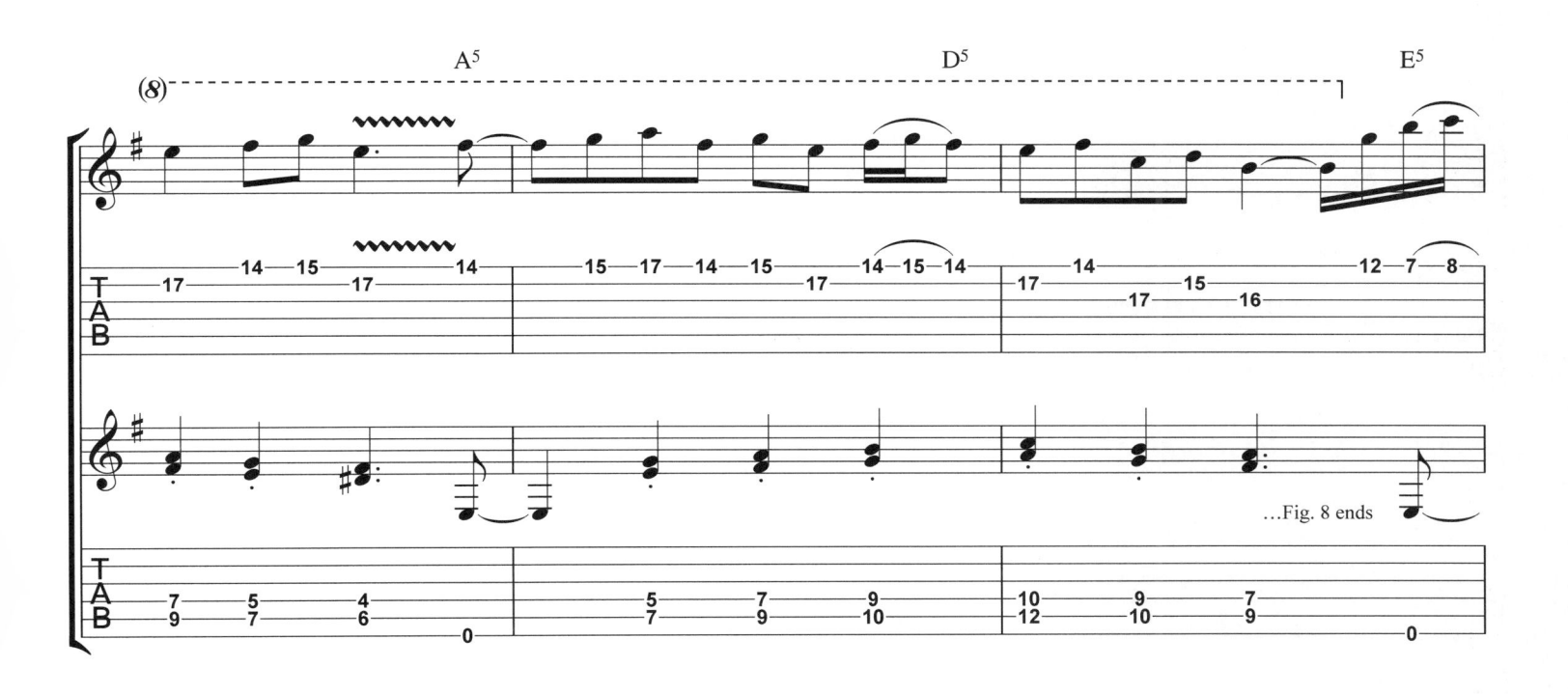

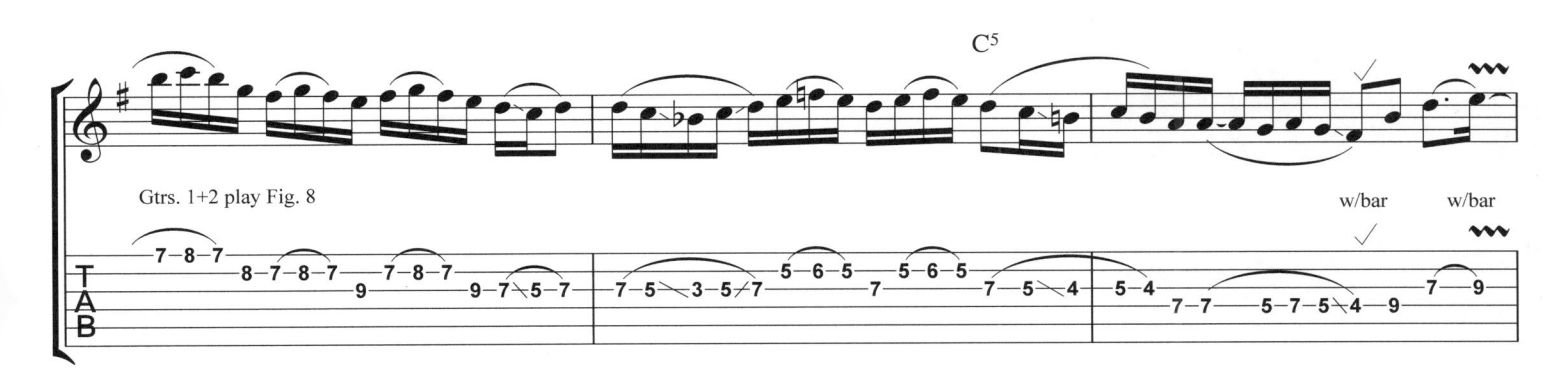

B5
3
3
A5
full
D5
E5
full
full
Gtrs. 1+2
Interlude
1° only
C5
B5
Gtr. 4 tacet
A5
D5
1.
2.
E5

Chorus

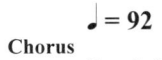

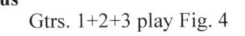

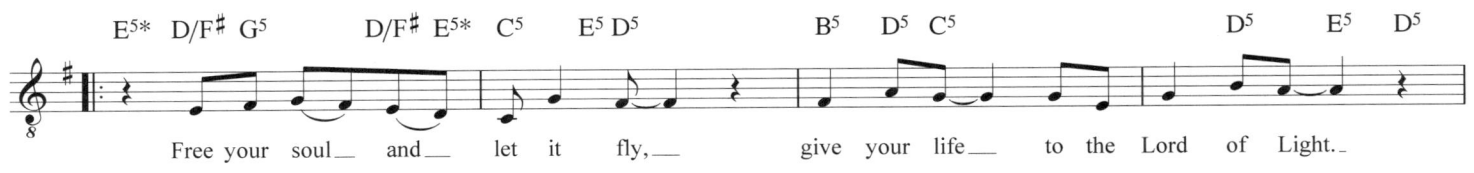

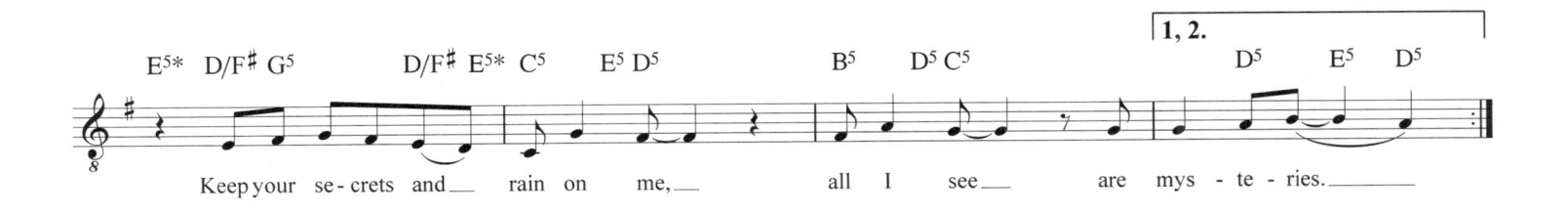

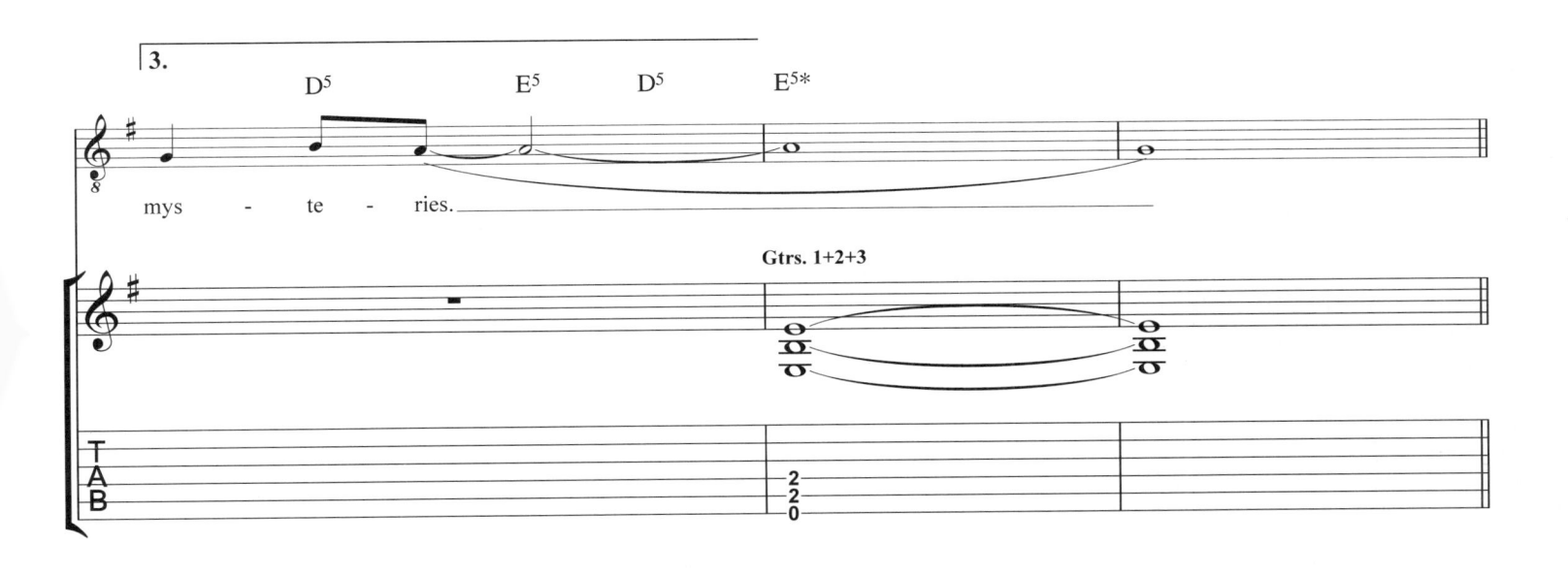

Free your soul and let it fly, give your life to the Lord of Light.

Keep your secrets and rain on me, all I see are mysteries.

mysteries.

THE LEGACY

Words & Music by Janick Gers & Steve Harris

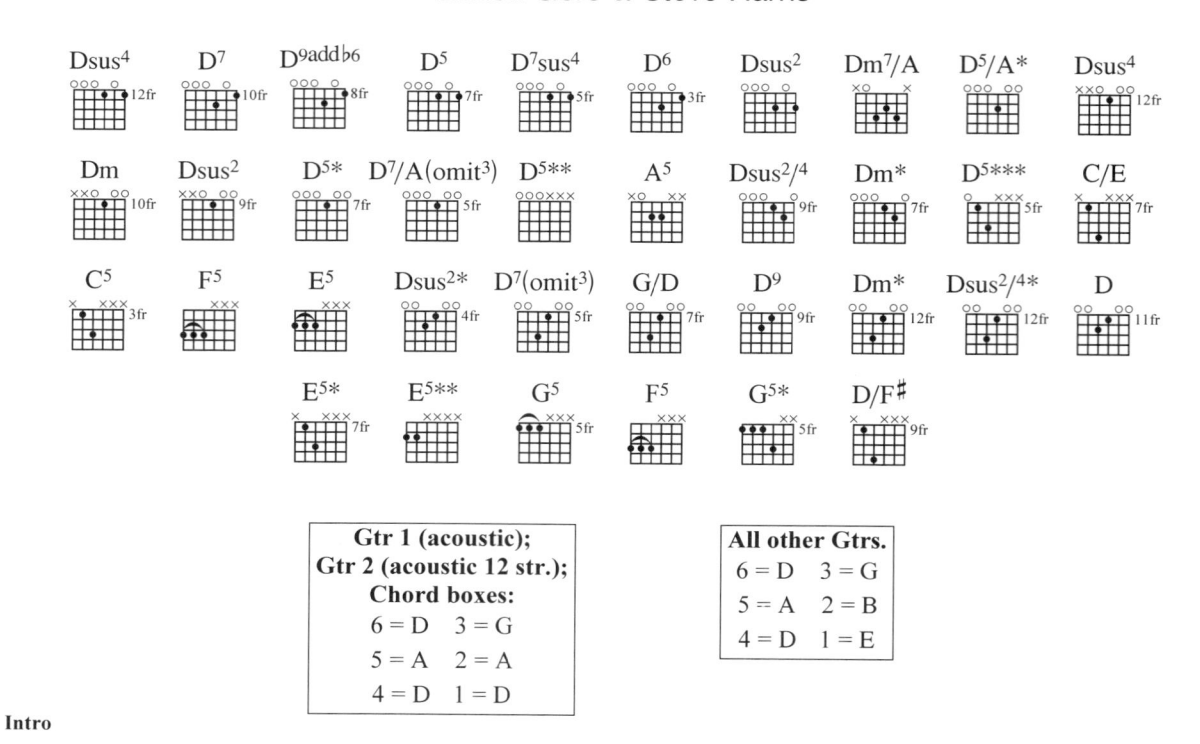

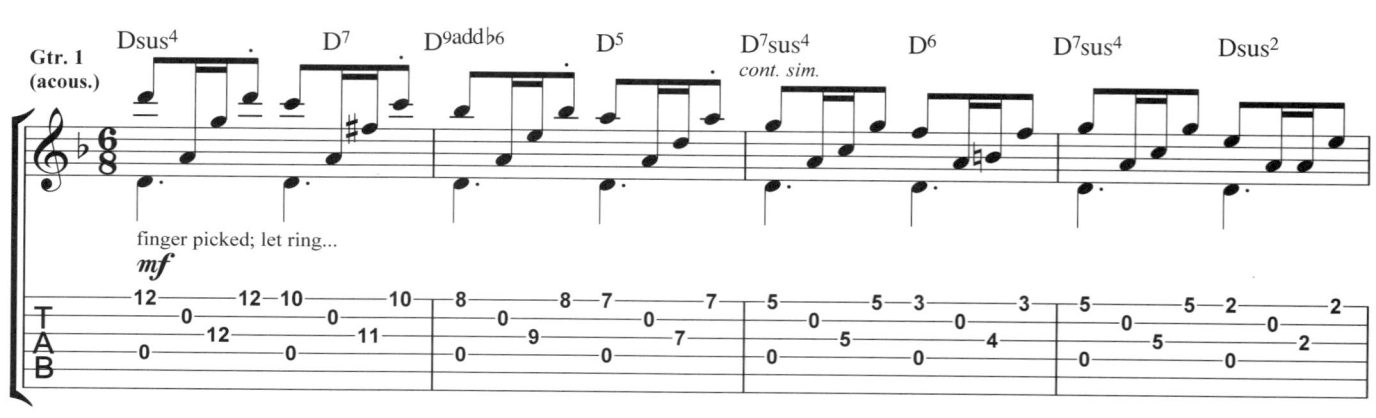

© Copyright 2006 Iron Maiden Publishing (Overseas) Limited.
BMG Music Publishing Limited.
All Rights Reserved. International Copyright Secured.

Verse
Dsus4 D7 D9add♭6 D5 D7sus4 D6 D7sus4 Dsus2
1. Tell you a thing that you ought to know. Two min - utes of your time, then on you go. Tell
2. Off to war to play lit - tle games, and on their re - turn, can't name no names. Some
Fig. 1
Gtr. 1 plays Fig. 1
Dsus4 D7 D9add♭6 D5 D7sus4 D6
tale of the men all dressed in black, that most of them, not
strange yel - low gas has played with their minds, has red - dened their eyes, re -
1.
2.
D7sus4 Dsus2 D7sus4 Dsus2 Dsus4 D7
com - ing back. 2. Sent - moved all the lies. As strange as it sounds, death
D9add♭6 D5 D7sus4 D6 D7sus4 Dsus2
knows no bounds. How ma - ny get well, on - ly time will tell.
Dsus4 D7 D9add♭6 D5 D7sus4 D6 D7sus4 Dsus2
rall.
Dsus2 D6 Dsus2 Dm7/A Dsus2 D6 Dsus2 D5*
On ly time will tell.

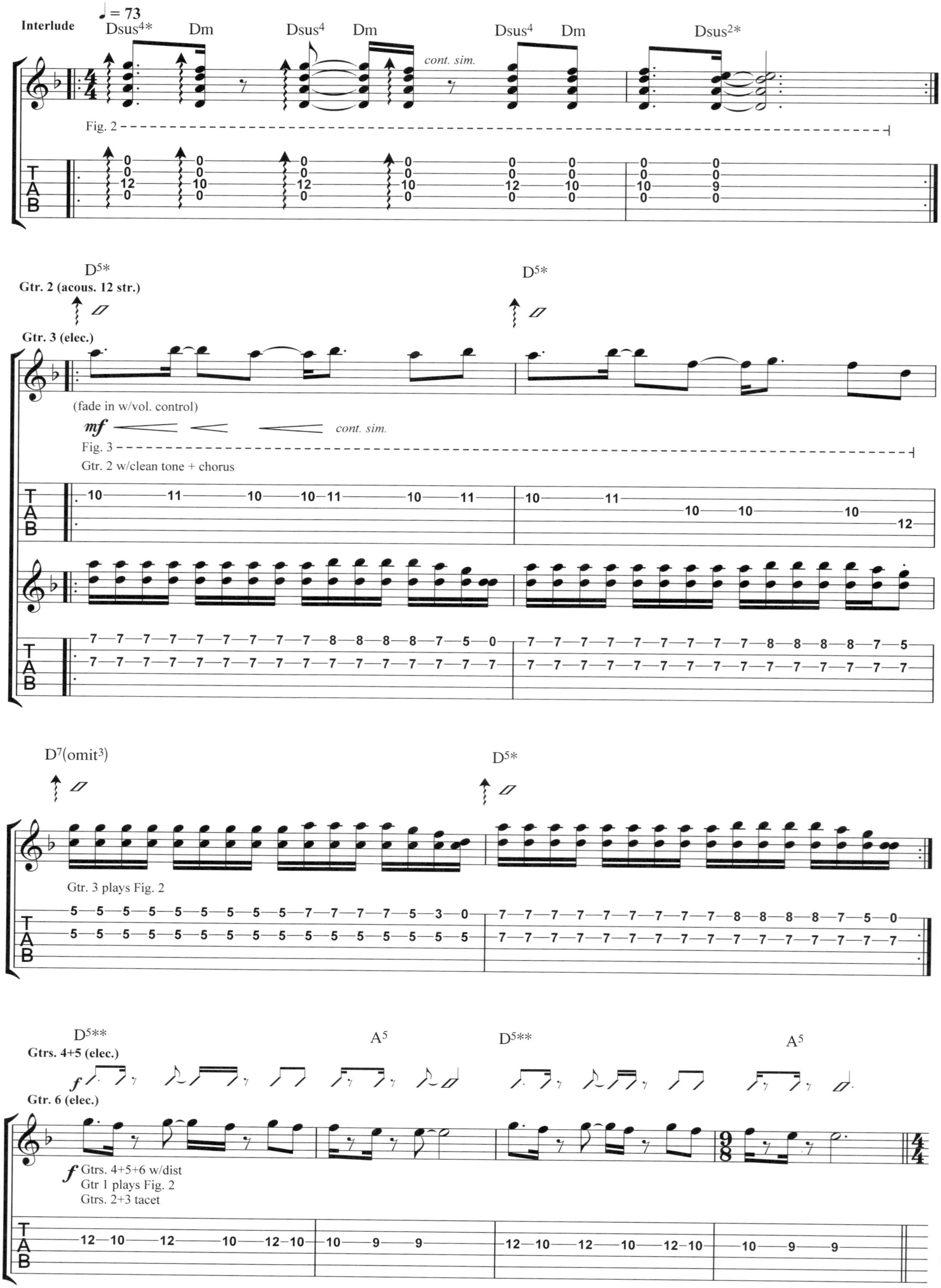
Interlude
♩ = 73
Dsus4* Dm Dsus4 Dm Dsus4 Dm Dsus2*
cont. sim.
Fig. 2
D5* D5*
Gtr. 2 (acous. 12 str.)
Gtr. 3 (elec.)
(fade in w/vol. control)
mf
cont. sim.
Fig. 3
Gtr. 2 w/clean tone + chorus
D7(omit3) D5*
Gtr. 3 plays Fig. 2
D5** A5 D5** A5
Gtrs. 4+5 (elec.)
Gtr. 6 (elec.)
f
Gtrs. 4+5+6 w/dist
Gtr 1 plays Fig. 2
Gtrs. 2+3 tacet

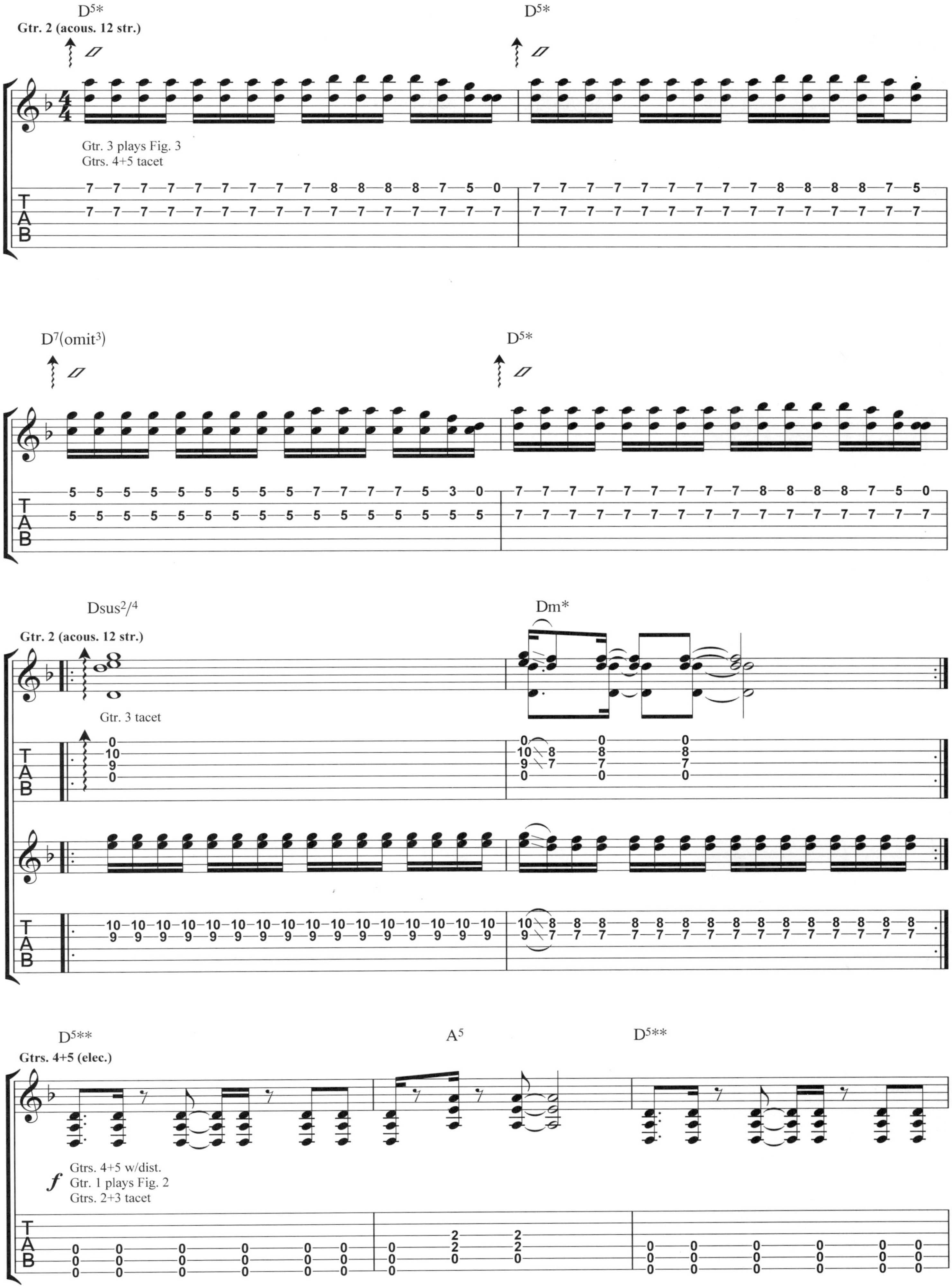
D5*
Gtr. 2 (acous. 12 str.)
D5*
Gtr. 3 plays Fig. 3
Gtrs. 4+5 tacet
D7(omit3)
D5*
Dsus2/4
Gtr. 2 (acous. 12 str.)
Dm*
Gtr. 3 tacet
D5**
Gtrs. 4+5 (elec.)
A5
D5**
f
Gtrs. 4+5 w/dist.
Gtr. 1 plays Fig. 2
Gtrs. 2+3 tacet

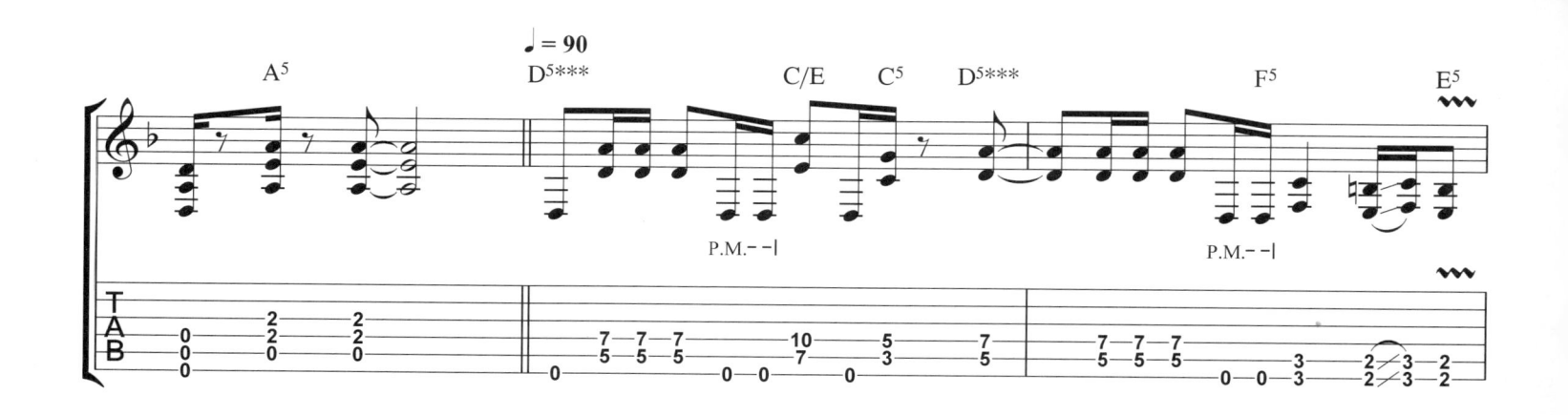

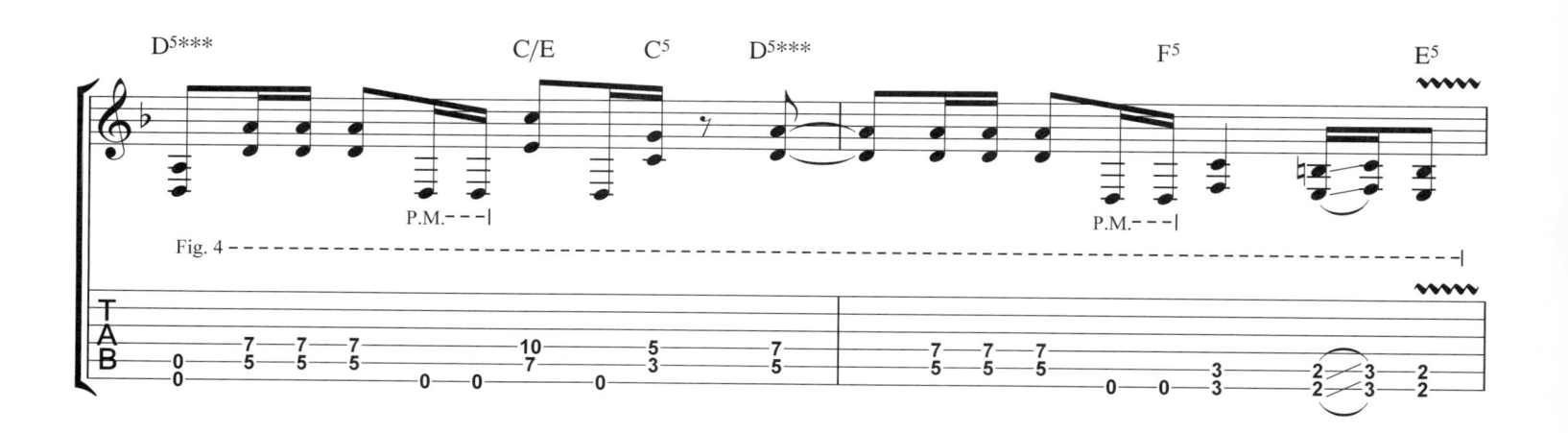

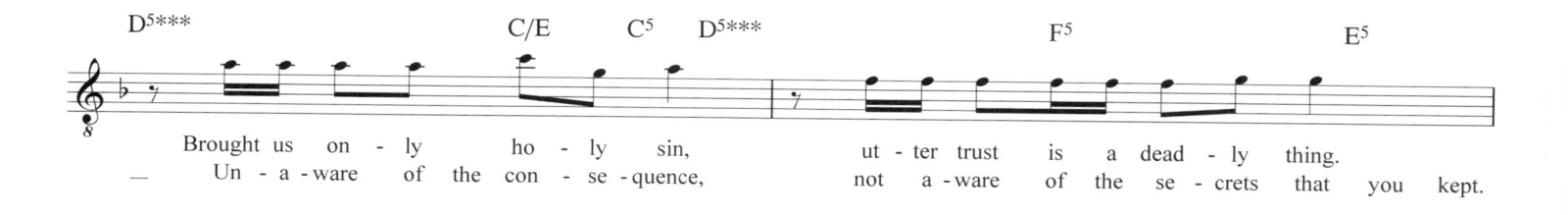

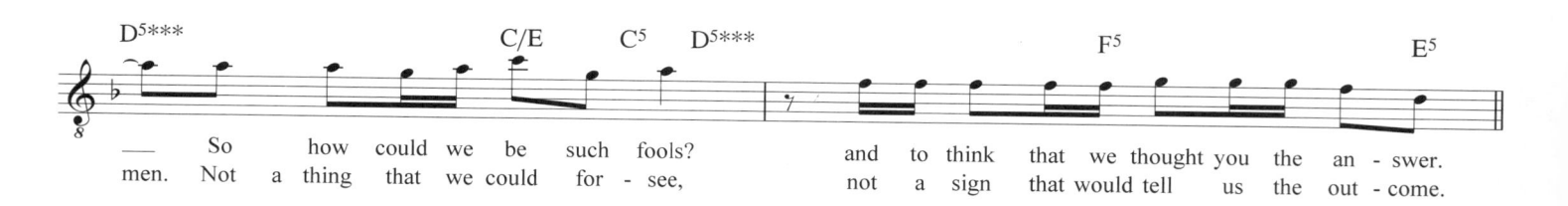

1. You lie in your death bed now, but what did you bring to the table?
2. Tang-led up in a web of lies, could have been a way to pro-phe-sise.

Brought us on-ly ho-ly sin, ut-ter trust is a dead-ly thing.
Un-a-ware of the con-se-quence, not a-ware of the se-crets that you kept.

To the prayer of ho-ly peace, we did-n't know what was ly-ing un-der-neath.
No-thing that we can't be-lieve, to re-veal the fa-cade of face-less

So how could we be such fools? and to think that we thought you the an-swer.
men. Not a thing that we could for-see, not a sign that would tell us the out-come.

Pre-Chorus
D5**
Dsus2*
I can't be - gin to un - der - stand - ing all the lies,
You had us all strung out with pro - mis - es of
Gtrs. 4+5
P.M.
Fig. 5
Gtrs. 1+2 (acous.)
D7(omit3)*
G/D
but on your death - bed I can see it in your eyes.
peace, but all a - long your cov - er plan was to de - ceive.
Gtrs. 4+5 play Fig. 5
D9
Dm*
Dsus2/4*
Just as clear as all the sweat up - on your brow, it real - ly makes
Can it put to rights now, on - ly time will tell, your pro - phe - cies

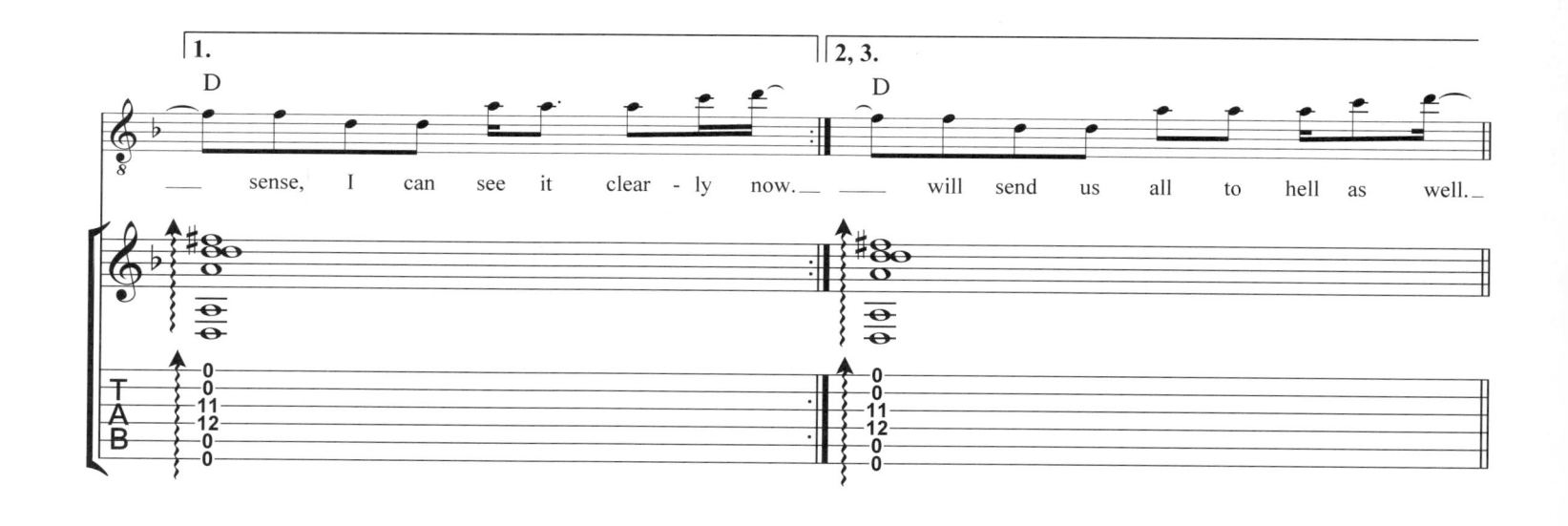

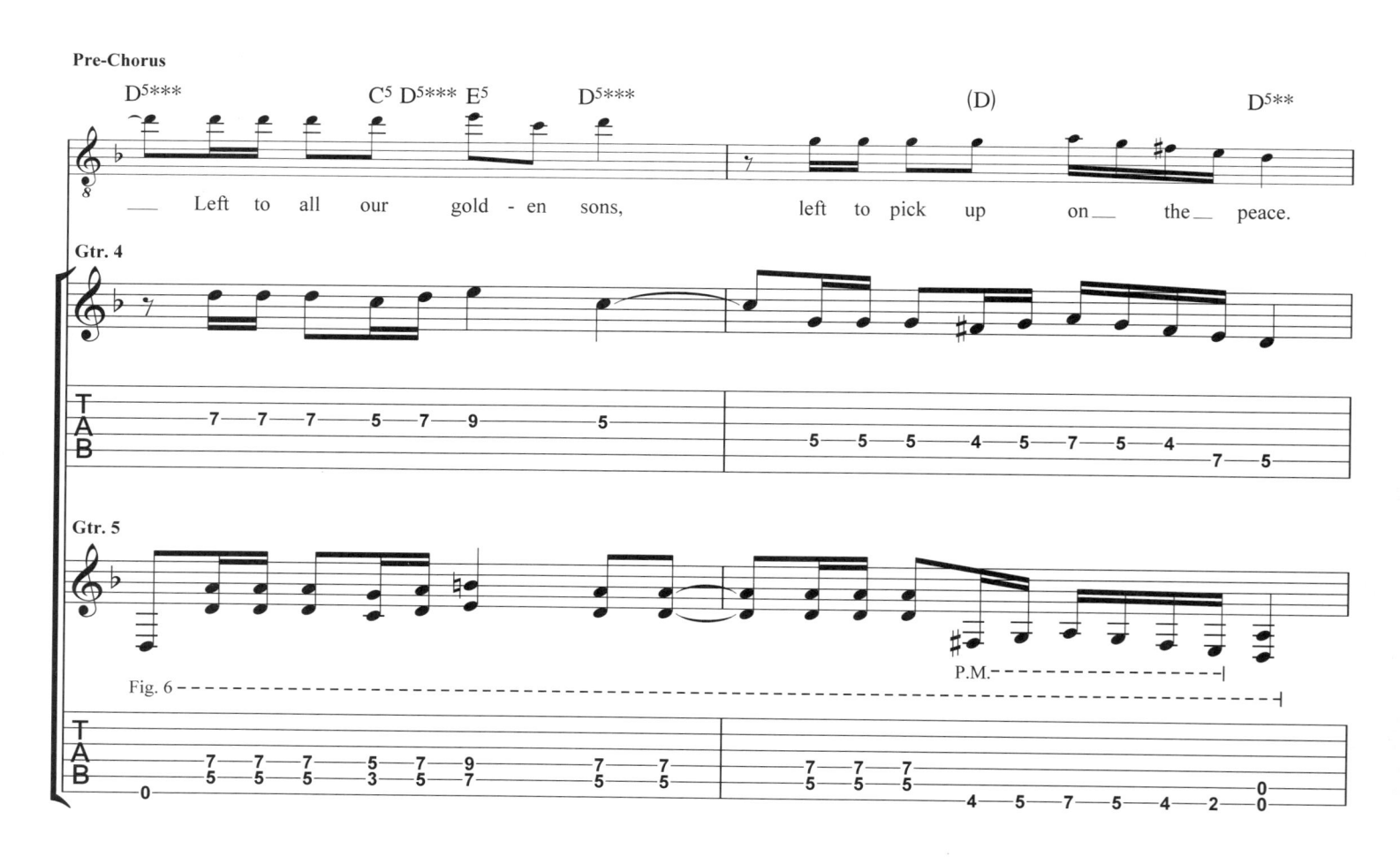

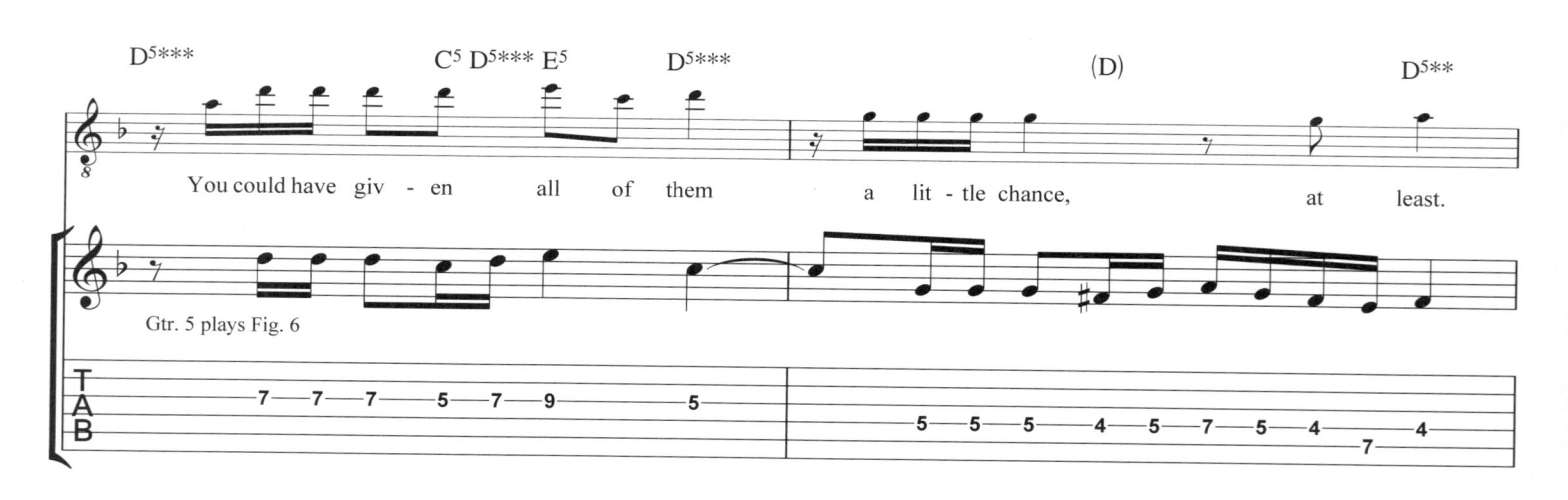

sense, I can see it clear - ly now.___ will send us all to hell as well.___

Pre-Chorus

Left to all our gold - en sons, left to pick up on the peace.

You could have giv - en all of them a lit - tle chance, at least.

D5*** C5 D5*** E5 D5*** (D) D5**
Take the world to a bet - ter place, giv - en them all just a lit - tle hope.
D5***
Gtr. 5
D5*** C5 D5*** E5 D5*** (D)
Just think, what a le - ga - cy, you now… will leave.
Interlude
♩= 73
D5** A5 D5** A5
Gtr. 6 (elec.)
Gtrs. 4+5 (elec.)
f w/dist.
♩. = 144
(D)
Gtr. 7 (elec.)
P.M.
Fig. 7…
Gtrs. 4+5+6 tacet

106

Gtr. Solo
D5** E5* C5 D5*** A5 D5** E5* C5
8va
Gtrs. 4+5 play Fig. 8
full
D5*** G5 D5** E5* C5 D5*** A5
tr
P.H.
G5
D5** E5* C5 D5*** A5
D5** E5* C5 D5*** G5
1/2

Interlude

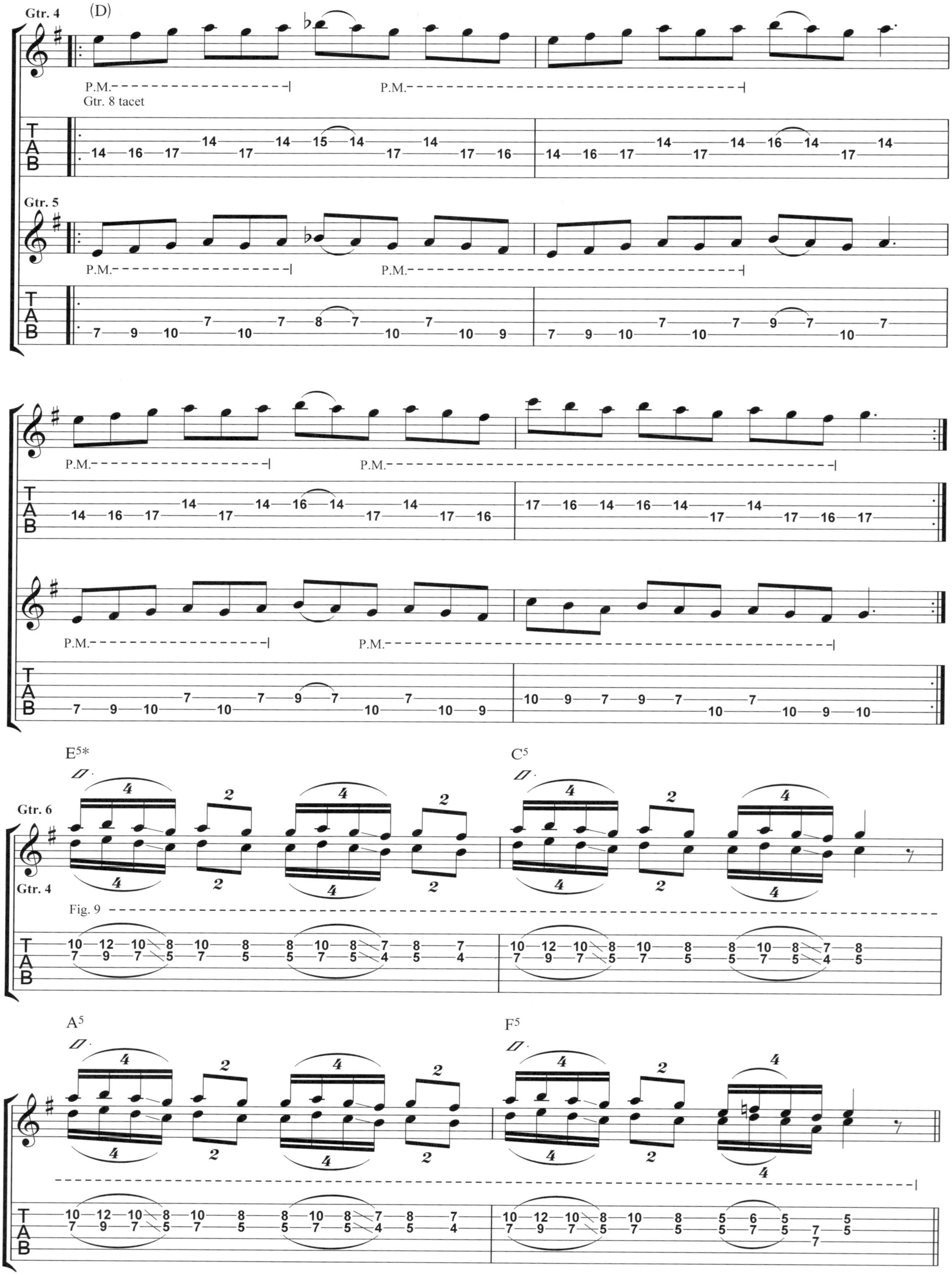

Chorus

We seem destined to live in fear, and some that would say armageddon is near. But where there's a life, well there's hope, that man won't self-destruct.

1. Why can't we treat our fellow men with more respect and a shake of their hands? But anger and loathing is rife, the death on all sides is becoming a way of
2. But some are just not wanting peace, their whole lives death and misery. The only thing that they learn, fight fire with fire, life is cheap.

109

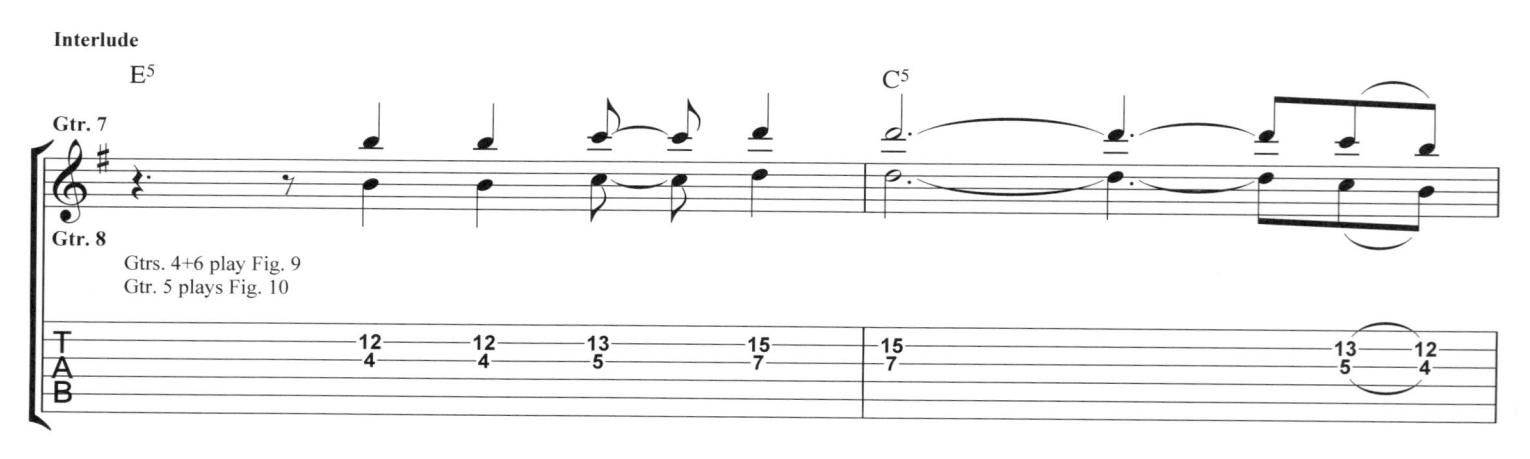

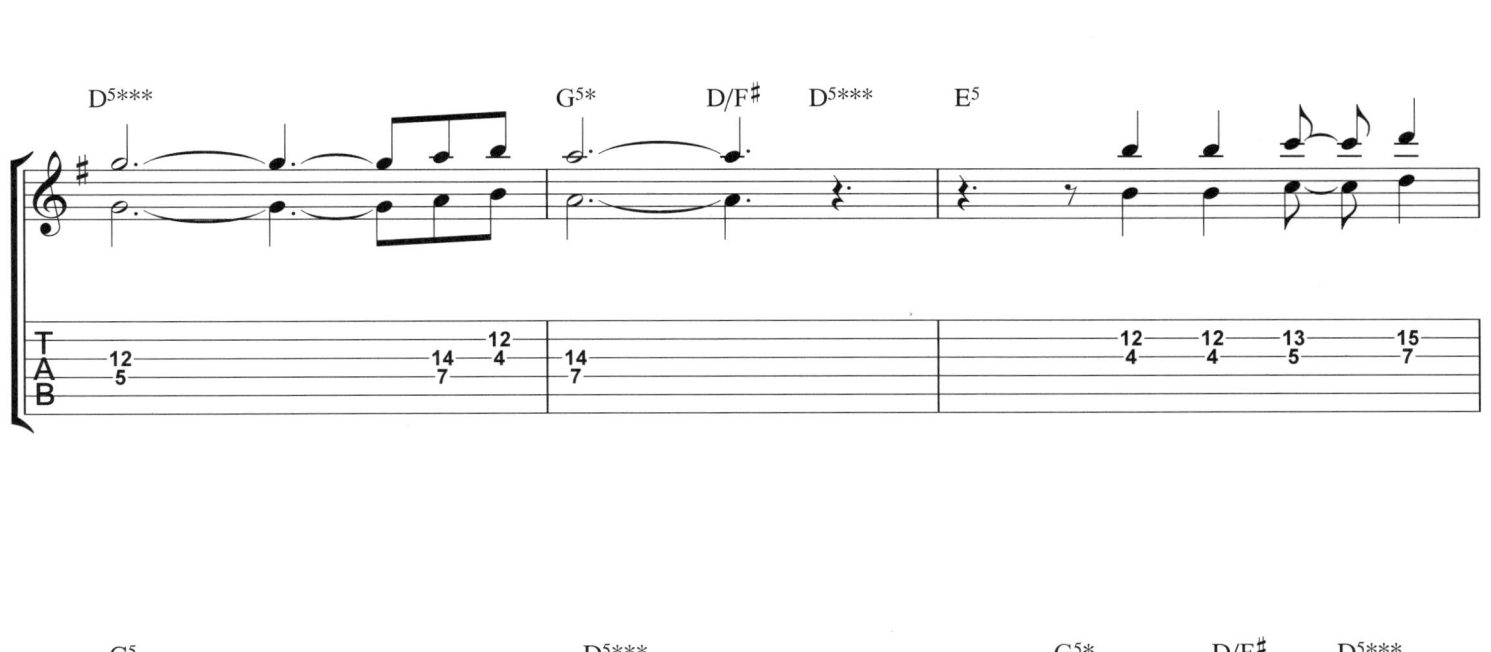

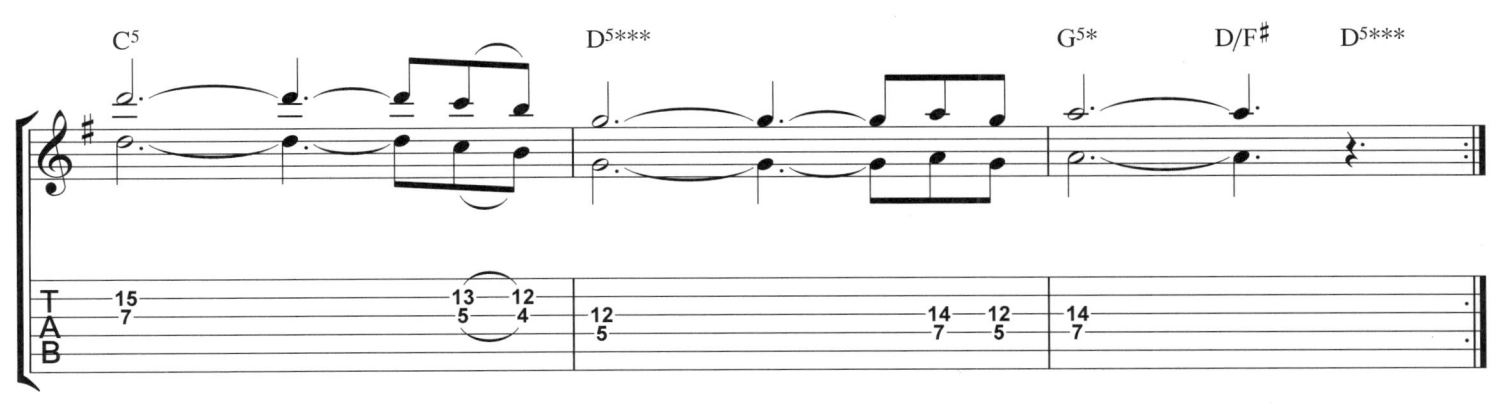

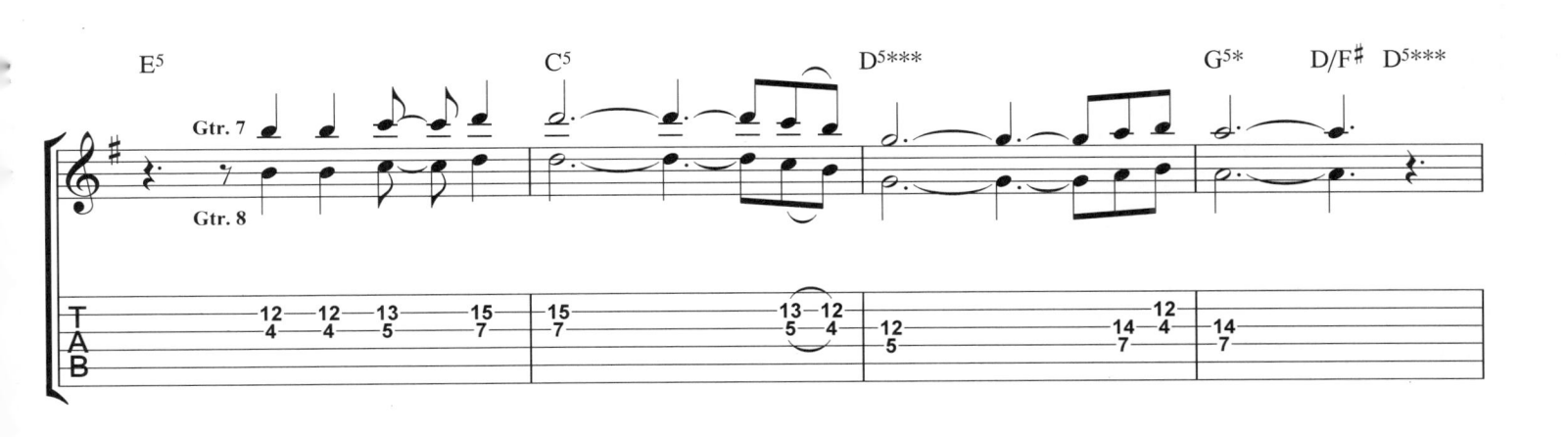

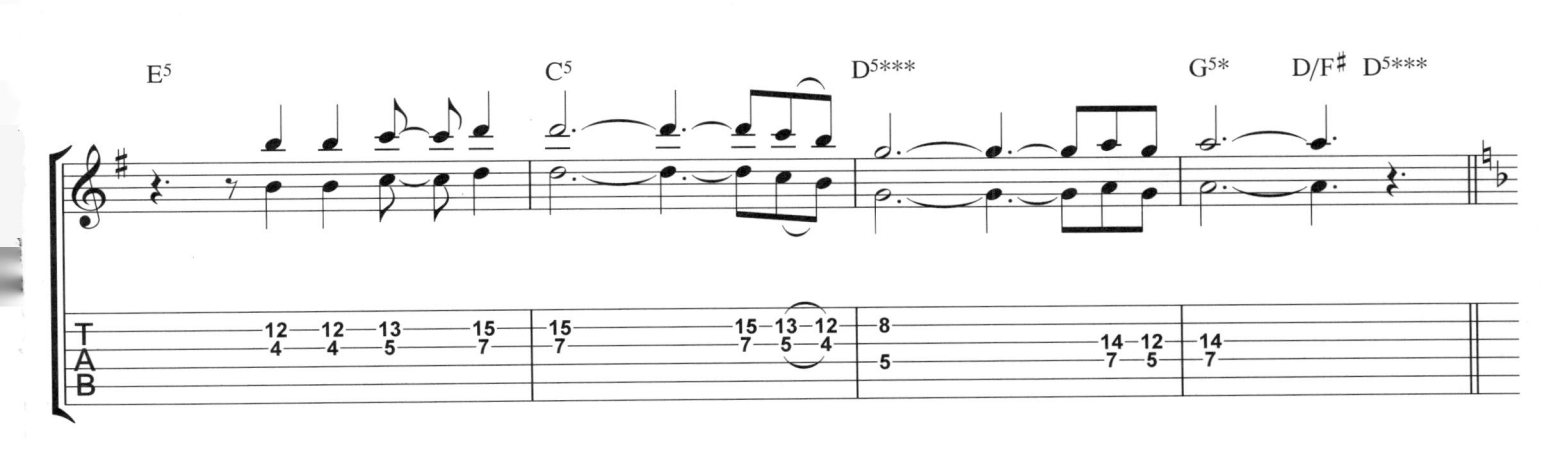

Gtr. 4
(D)
P.M.
Gtrs. 6, 7+8 tacet
Gtr. 5
1.
2.
rall.
Outro
♩ = 63
Gtr. 2 (acous. 12 str.)
Dsus4* Dm Dsus4 Dm Dsus4 Dm Dsus2*
Dsus4* Dm Dsus4 Dm Dsus4 Dm Dsus2* D5*

1 2 3 4 5 6 7 8 9